Part One
Blue Ridge Summit
The Beginnings of a Resort Area

Part Two
Colonial Counterfeiters
of the Blue Ridge

by
John Howard McClellan

Copyright @ 2007 by John Howard McClellan
All Rights Reserved
All photographs copyrighted to John Howard McClellan
Unless otherwise credited

This 2007 Edition is the 2nd printing of a combined volume
1. Blue Ridge Summit, The Beginnings of a Resort Era
An historical paper presented May 25, 1982
Copyrighted @ 1982- LC 83 105292
F159. B644 M23 1982- 974.8/44.20
1. Resorts 2. Blue Ridge Summit—History
2. Blue Ridge Summit, (PA)—History
2. Colonial Counterfeiters of the Blue Ridge
An historical paper presented November 17, 1989
Copyrighted @ 1989 LCMLCM 92/08382 (F)
1. Counterfeiters, Pennsylvania
2. Blue Ridge Counterfeiters—History

Library of Congress Cataloging-in-Publication Data
John Howard McClellan 1927-
Blue Ridge Summit. The beginnings of a resort era
John Howard McClellan
Colonial Counterfeiters of the Blue Ridge
John Howard McClellan
p.   cm.
Includes illustrations & bibliographical references

2nd Printing

ISBN 978-0-9790983-1-4
Manufactured in the United States of America

Copyquik Printing and Graphics, LLC
710 Oak Hill Avenue, Hagerstown, MD. 21740
www.copyquik.com

Blue Ridge Summit
The Beginnings of a Resort Area

(Part One)

by
John Howard McClellan

Blue Ridge Summit
(The Beginnings of a Resort Area)

Part One was originally presented
before the
Kittochtinny Historical Society
Chambersburg, Franklin County, Pennsylvania
May 25, 1982

Copyright © 1982 - John Howard McClellan

This 2002 edition was printed by
Copyquik Printing and Graphics, LLC
710 Oak Hill Avenue, Hagerstown, MD 21740

Manufactured in the United States of America

Library of Congress Cataloging Data

McClellan, John Howard, 1927-
   Blue Ridge Summit, the beginnings of a resort era/John Howard McClellan
     p.   cm.
   Includes bibliographical references
   LC 83 105292
   1. Resorts, 2. Blue Ridge Summit—History
   2. Blue Ridge Summit (PA)—History
   F159.B644 M23 1982
   974.8/44,20

Cover sketch by Lester Jay Stone, 1976
printed with permission of the
Blue Ridge Summit Free Library, Blue Ridge Summit, PA 17214

Accompanying photographs copyrighted to
John Howard McClellan, unless otherwise credited.
All Rights Reserved. 1982

Acknowledgements

I would like to acknowledge the important role that librarians and archivists, everywhere, play in the advancement of historical research and new knowledge in all fields of endeavor. These librarians, keepers of the word, labor diligently at a thankless and often boring job for little pay and little else, but the satisfaction of knowing that they, alone, may find it, when no one else can!

I would, most seriously propose, that, in addition to National Library Week; our nation, observe a *National Librarian's Week*. There are not now, nor ever have been libraries without librarians!

The staff members and interested individuals, following, offered their assistance to me on numerous occasions, many times without being asked.

Alexander Hamilton Free Library- Ruth Baer Gembe, Pamela Coyle
Blue Ridge Summit Free Library–Carol Bailey
Coyle Free Library, Hamilton Library of Cumberland County Historical Society; Dickinson College Library.
Ezra Lehman Library, Shippensburg State College–Fred Smith, Mrs. Barbara Taylor
Md. Dept. of Enoch Pratt Library–Morgan Pritchett
Franklin County, PA. Courthouse–David Bowers, John L. George, Fred Kraiss, George Heefner, Lorraine Royer and Glenn Shadle
Kittochtinny Historical Society–Homer T. Rosenberger, Lillian Colletta, Janet Z. Gabler
Maryland Historical Society–Laurie Baty, Eric Vbalsvic
Penna Historical and Museum Commission–Martha Simmonetti, John Shelly, Lillian Ulrich
Washington County (MD) Free Library–John and Dennis Frey

Individuals–Harvey C. Bridgers, Jr., Kenton H. Broyles, Harold and Dorothy Gingrich, W. Kenneth and Joanne C. Haugh, Harry R. McClain, Charles L. Pague, Mary F. Harbaugh Peiffer, Robert R. Peiffer, C. Omar Tracey, C. Anderson Warner, O. E. Weikert, Jr. G. Fred Zeigler. A special thanks to Tammy Price Miller.

Special Acknowledgement

To my wife, Pauline Ness Johnston and sons, John, Thomas Brian, Robert and Richard, without whose love, patience, kindness, fortitude and understanding this paper would not have ever been written. A special thanks to John for photographic work; to Thomas and Robert for editing and research; to Richard for special research on Buena Vista area and to Brian for his interest and encouragement.

Dedication

This paper is the fruition of a quarter century long dream that began on the day I met the man to whom this paper is respectfully dedicated:

Charles S. Gardner, Jr. (1907-1964)

He was a native and life-long resident of Blue Ridge Summit. He was a member of Kittochtinny Historical Society and encouraged and sponsored me to membership. His historic intelligence, his enjoyment of life and his joy in the discovery of new historic facts was gratifying to behold.

BLUE RIDGE SUMMIT
(The Beginnings of a Resort Area)

The Blue Ridge Summit community lies at the top of the South Mountain. A community that stretches its environs into parts of four counties and two states, straddling the Mason Dixon line. On the Pennsylvania side, it lies in parts of Franklin and Adams counties. On the Maryland side of the line, it extends into both Frederick and Washington counties. The subject of our study lies in the southeastern corner of Franklin County, Pennsylvania, in the Township of Washington.

After the introduction of the railroad in 1872, this area grew to become a lively and fashionable vacation community. Near the turn of the last century, this region was in its hey-day. It remained a resort area until its decline during the Depression of 1929 and the following years of limited travel, during World War II (1939-1945).

There has been little documented on the full century preceding the fashionable period of the colorful 1890's in this locale. To view its origin and development seems a worthwhile endeavor for those interested in the past.

Tradition tells us that these mountains were traversed by the Indians of the Woodland Epoch, such as, the Susquehannock or Conestogoe Tribes of the Delaware Nation and the Tuscarora of the Cherokee Nation. The Indians used paths over these mountains close to Mt. Dunlap and Clermont Crag. Continuous use of these paths by the Indians in their interactions with each other pioneered the courses of early roads through Blue Ridge Summit.

Blue Ridge Summit was not always so-called. It spreads out over a gap in the South Mountain which was aptly named South Gap.[1] This gap became the convergency of major thoroughfares into and out of the "Great Valleys": those being the Cumberland Valley of Pennsylvania and Maryland, and the Shenandoah Valley of Virginia.

Of these converging roads, one of the most important colonial highways crossed through this Gap. It was referred to on Scull's *Map of Pennsylvania of 1759* as "The Great Waggon Road to Philadelphia" or "The Great Road from Yadkin River thro Virginia to Philadelphia distance 435 miles." The great road began at Philadelphia and went through Lancaster and York, crossed through the gap at Blue Ridge Summit, then on to Hagerstown. From Hagerstown it continued to Williamsport, Winchester, Staunton, crossed the James River, then southwest to the Yadkin River, near Winston-Salem, North Carolina. It is here that Boone's Wilderness Road started west through Tennessee and Kentucky.[2] This early highway was the major traffic artery in colonial times from the ports of Philadelphia and New Jersey to points in Ohio,

---

1 *Map of Pennsylvania,* N. Scull, 1775.
2 Albert C. Rose, *Historic American Roads,* Crown, N.Y. 1976.

the Northwest and Southwest territories. Other converging roads were of local origin. One being conceived by petition of the inhabitants of Peters Township in the County of Cumberland who petitioned the Court in 1761 to allow a road from John McDowell's mill (present day Markes) and William Smith's mill (Mercersburg) to meet at or near William Maxwell's (near Upton) and on toward Baltimore town until it intersected the York County line. The court promptly appointed viewers, whom after six years had failed to act. Again, the inhabitants petitioned and the court reappointed viewers.

On April 15, 1768, the viewers reported to Cumberland County Court of Quarter Sessions that they had viewed the mills. They allowed that the two roads from the mills should meet at or near James Irwin's (Irwin Mills), in Peters Township, instead of William Maxwell's, then to cross the Conococheague (East Branch) near the mouth of Muddy Run (Rt. 16 near Greencastle) through Antrim Township to the *Gap in the South Mountain*. This route they imagined was the most direct course to Baltimore. The viewers also allowed that the same road was a good wagon road and would be of public advantage to the greatest part of the upper end of the county. From the two mills westward, the viewers agreed to "Briddle Road" for the accommodation of Air and Fannett Townships.[3]

The Gap, named Nicholson's Gap, was probably so called because it led out of the Cumberland Valley toward *Nicholson's Manor*, a 1674 Baltimore County land grant of over 4000 acres to

---

3 *Quarter Sessions Docket #1*, Cumberland County, Clerk of Courts, p. 138, April Quarter Sessions, 1768.

Sir Francis Nicholson, who was a patron of learning and municipal improvement in Colonial Maryland.

On the York County side of South Mountain this Gap was known as "Willoughby's Gap." It was probably named after Willoughby Winchester who received a grant, September 11, 1734 for lands located at "Spring Meadows" at the junction of Willoughby's Run and Marsh Creek in what is now Adams County.[4]

There were other roads through Nicholson's Gap which should be noted. The Georgetown or Middletown Valley Road was an early route through Nicholson Gap by Mt. Zion, through Middletown and Frederick and into Georgetown, now Washington, D.C. The Chambersburg-Baltimore Road led through the Nunnery, Tomstown, Mentzer Gap and intersected the Baltimore Road near Nicholson's. Often these roads were laid out and opened by private citizens for the benefit of local commerce.[5]

Along these early roads, through our mountains, were scattered the primitive improvements of our first residents, who had traveled far with hopes of starting a life of freedom. Although the farmland along the Blue Ridge was not very fertile, being either too rocky or too sandy, many tried their hand at farming. Some stayed and survived by clearing patches of land for a cabin and garden. They adapted to conditions by "half-farming" and earned a living by laboring at other pursuits

---

[4] Interview with *Charles Glatfelter,* Adams County Historical Society, March 27, 1982.

[5] *Quarter Sessions Docket #1,* Cumberland County, Clerk of Courts, Pg 134, April Session 1774.

such as hunting, timbering, bark-peeling, charcoaling, wagon driving, tanning and shoemaking. Their humble homes became inns, and unknowingly they became the hosts of our first resorts.

Weary travellers along the colonial roads needed a place to rest themselves, their mounts, teams, and droves, especially after reaching the summit of the Blue Ridge.

These early resting places were nothing more than the homes of settlers who took the wearied traveller in, accommodating them with what they had at hand. Most times the guest was given pot luck, a place to sleep on the floor and a little grain for his animals. The host, in good conscience, could not charge for this, his generosity born in the hope that he would be treated likewise when on the road. The guest, rising before daylight, generally left some-thing for the host's hospitality, and was gone, seeking his breakfast as he rested his animals at mid-morning. This practice resulted in many places to stop. Advertisement was by word of mouth.

The trials and tribulations of the traveller and host alike were many in those days. An interesting look at this type of resorting is furnished by this traveller in Pennsylvania in 1679-80 near Philadelphia:

> "This house is the highest up the river (Delaware) hitherto inhabited. Here we had to lodge; and although we were too tired to eat, we had to remain sitting upright the whole night, not being able to find room enough to lie upon the ground. We had a fire however, but the dwellings are so wretchedly constructed, that if you are not so close to the fire as almost to burn yourself, you can not keep

warm, for the wind blows through them every where...Now this house was new and airy; and as the night was windy from the north, I will not readily forget it."[6]

It was not exactly the Holiday Inn!

The earliest written reference to the Blue Ridge Summit area, we find, is in the *Journal of Phillip Vickers Fithian,* an itinerant minister. He was born in New Jersey, educated at Princeton, studied theology, and was ordained by the Presbytery of Philadelphia. Since there were no open pulpits in the thickly populated areas of New Jersey and Pennsylvania, he began, in May 1775, just at the outset of the American Revolution, to ride a "circuit" as a missionary into what he called the "frontiers."

To suggest that Blue Ridge Summit, much less any of that which is now Franklin County, was a frontier in 1775 was hardly accurate, although Fithian did reach some distinctly primitive outposts. By this time, the frontier had been pushed as far as Fort Pitt and westward. Fithian was a keen observer and a clever, interesting writer. In his diary, that was written clear, in concise English, there is little that can be misinterpreted. He showed a ready sense of humor and an understanding of worldly ways hardly expected of one so young, particularly a man of the cloth.

Mr. Fithian first visited our part of the country in the company of a fellow novice clergyman, Andrew Hunter. He came from Philadelphia by way of Lancaster and stating of

---

6   Dr. Henry C. Mercer, "Origin of Log Houses in the U.S.," Bucks County Historical Society, Doylestown, Penna., 1924, p. 578.

Yorktowne (present day York, Pa.) in his journal on May 16, 1775: "Its inhabitants are all Dutch." Meaning that they were chiefly of German extraction.

Pressing on west the following morning, Fithian exclaims:

> "Look Andrew, how very remote we can see a hill before us! That is the South Blue Mountain-It looks like the border of a Black cloud raised a very little above the trees! It is now thirty miles off..."[7]

He and Mr. Hunter reached the summit of our Blue Ridge on May 18, 1775, which he had called the South Blue Mountain. Actually it is just the South Mountain. The Blue Mountain being shown by Scull's Map of 1775 as part of the Kittatinny range farther to the north. Upon arriving at the top of the South Mountain, Mr. Fithian writes in his journal:

> "Here we arrived, late last night, at a small log house—A smart, neat, young, Landlady; a spry, golden haird buxom Maid; several-sturdy waggoner; Huge hills on every side; A Vast distance from Home; Mr. Hunter very unwell—I had, indeed, like afflicted Job, a "Night of Tossing...!" We are at what is called, "Nicholson's Gap"—Mr. Hunter is better and we jogg on over the ragged Hills—A middle aged dropsical Dutch woman, with her face muffled up in the Mumps, boild up for our breakfast, a little coffee, in the Sugar and Milk, it made a good Broth—! From the Mountain to Elizabeth's or Hager's Town is a level Country and a Good land."[8]

Here we have it, on good authority, from Phillip Vickers Fithian, a walking, talking Reverend gentleman; that he, in the

---

7   R.G. Albion and L. Dodson (eds.), *Journal of Phillip Vickers Fithian 1775-1776*, (Princeton Univ. Press, 1934), p. 7.
8   Ibid, p. 9.

company of another, in the year 1775, lodged along with some wagoners, at a log house of a neat landlady, the housekeeper of an inn at Nicholson's Gap, (Blue Ridge Summit). We lament the fact that he tells us no more of conditions there. We can assume they were satisfactory from his praise of his landlady's neatness, by reason that he was, at other times, quick to record in his journal unsatisfactory circumstances encountered. Accommodation at Nicholson's seemed to be, at least, *adequate* by Fithian's standards even though he spent the night in tossing.

We would like to believe that he and Mr. Hunter had stopped at the *Maguire Place,* at *Bubbling Spring.* This was part of a large tract owned by Daniel Royer, whose extensive tannery, hemp mill, and grist mill then occupied the site of the present Renfrew Museum, east of Waynesboro, Pa.

The Bubbling Spring, between old Route 16 and the Sunshine Trail, (new Route 16), is now a source of water supply for the Washington Township Municipal Authority. The Appalachian Trail crosses the site diagonally, in close proximity, to the old building foundations and the spring, which is now enclosed. This spring was a sand spring from which entrapped air was released to the surface in a myriad of bubbles. It is still a spring of considerable purity and flow. The spring lies at the western terminus of the legendary "Devil's Race Course" of Pennsylvania. This geologic oddity was the subject of a paper presented before this Society on February 22, 1979 by our colleague Becky Dietrich.[9]

In fact, the "Devil's Race Course" rock formation, which was a

---

[9] Becky Dietrich, "The Summit Plateau-Story," *Kittochtinny Historical Society Papers,* XVII, pp. 71-93.

large boulder field devoid of trees before it was crushed and used as base fill for the construction of new Route 16 in 1939, was probably the reason that John Maguire moved down the valley, approximately a mile, to buy part of a Maryland grant called "Brandywine Level." The land at Bubbling Spring was rocky, barren and absolutely nonproductive. The buildings were small and consisted of a house built of round logs, 17 x 21 feet with three windows, a shed and small outbuilding.[10] Although the spring was good, pasture was non-existent and the location was cold in the winter with little sunshine.

There was talk of a new road, a turnpike. It was time to move and find more productive land which could be farmed, with pasture that could be enclosed for the herds and teams that passed daily to the city markets.

John Maguire's decision to move proved wise, because where he built his new wagonstand, on the bend of the road near a good spring, was a considerable improvement over the former stand. It was probably constructed of lumber cut at the sawmill of Daniel Royer, in the vale just below the road. The new building was of frame construction, 16 rooms with washrooms at the end of the hall, a dining room and barroom, and a long porch where laughing wagoners could test each others whips, try the cards and dice, wrestle or box, and raise old Nick. This establishment stood near a spring on the southside of Old Route 16 at its intersection with Buena Vista Road.[11]

---

10 *Tax Evaluation Docket #1, Franklin County, Pa.,* Clerk of Courts Office, Franklin County, Pa.
11 Public Sale Advertisement, *Village Record,* March 30, 1866.

"Devil's Race Course" at Monterey
Wash. Twp., Franklin Co., PA.

This large boulder field was situated near Maguire's first tavern, near the "Bubbling Spring." It ran from the crossing of the (present) Appalachian Trail and New and Old Rts. 16, W. of Monterey Peak for some distance. Freezing, thawing and the action of gravity caused the ancient boulder accumulations to form this rock stream by action of "creep." The surface, devoid of trees, consisted of boulders so large and rough, they were difficult to walk over. This surface gave rise to the legend that the "Devil" was wont to foot.race over it. Some of this scenic oddity was removed for base fill in 1939 in the construction of New (present) Rt. 16.

The name Daniel Royer keeps appearing and reappearing in our study of the development of the South Mountain. He was an entrepreneur when it came to land titles. His experience as a tax assessor and census taker in Washington Township, probably gave him insight into the ownership and boundaries of land along the South Mountain. Royer first enumerated Maguire in the Pennsylvania census of 1807.[12] He counted John Maguire as an innkeeper. It was probably then and there he found, if he had not already known, that Maguire's Maryland grant was surrounded by a survey Royer had made on a Pennsylvania right in 1792. There was title interference. Royer needed the tanbark and lumber. Maguire wanted the spring and wagon stand. There is always more than one way to skin a cat! In 1813, they joined forces. The land was patented to John Maguire and Daniel Royer.[13]

In 1816, an act of incorporation was passed in the Pennsylvania Legislature forming the Waynesburg, Greencastle and Mercersburg Turnpike Company.[14] A paper discussing the formation and history of this company was presented before Kittochtinny Society on May 31, 1979 by our colleague, G. Fred Zeigler of Greencastle. On September 21, 1820, the road was reported completed over the mountain from the Maryland line near Emmitsburg to the west end of Waynesboro. It must have

---

12 *Septennial Census on Microfilm.* 1807, Pennsylvania Historical and Museum Commission, (PHMC).
13 Land Patent, C-143-38-328 Ac. 1812, App 875-1766 State Land Office, PHMC See Also D-37-287, 275 Ac. 1792.
14 G. Fred Zeigler, "The Waynesburg, Green-castle and Mercersburg Turnpike," *Kittochtinny Historical Society Papers,* Vol. XVII, Chambersburg, Pa., 1981.

been a fairly good road to begin with, if the mountainous section was finished so quickly. Whether the company could collect tolls or not made no difference to Maguire. A good road increased his business.

In 1821, scheduled post coaches for passengers were started from Hagerstown, Maryland to Gettysburg, Pennsylvania, and return. Stockton and Stokes, founders of the coach company hoped to accommodate persons traveling to Philadelphia or Wheeling, West Virginia. These coaches passed along the new turnpike road close by Maguire's.[15]

At that time, however, there were needed accommodations for all types of travellers. The aristocrat, the mother with children, the banker and the businessman would only under direst circumstances sleep under the same roof with teamsters and drovers. There were connected with such places many stories of robbery, murder and mysterious disappearances.

To attract the "carriage trade," Maguire, in partnership with Royer, Martin Funk and others built a new and larger inn, south of the wagon stand on the hill overlooking a spectacular view of the Cumberland Valley and the South Mountain ranges. This building was of more refined architecture, with a parlor and a dining room, bedrooms, some likely with curtained bedsteads, and bathrooms at the end of the hall. The business was there and the Cold Spring got it, both coming and going. John Maguire kept the wagon tavern, Martin Funk kept the inn.

Times and transportation were changing. The Chesapeake

---

15 J. Thomas Scharf, *History of Western Maryland*, Vol. II, Philadelphia, Pa., 1882 p. 1003.

and Ohio Canal played a part in changing the direction of trade and traffic, as did Pennsylvania's own canal system. The C & O headed passengers and shipping off at Cumberland, Maryland. The Pennsylvania Canal and Portage directed shipping and travel to Pittsburgh and then north of the Blue Ridge. The railroads were coming. The Baltimore and Ohio and The Philadelphia and Reading railroads, although slow in developing, were bidding for the same commerce.

In the 1847's, John Maguire moved to Allegheny County leaving the management of the old hostelry to his children and Joseph Funk.[16] Business was declining. The restorative powers of the baths and spring water began to be emphasized in advertisements.

From 1852 to 1856, the inn was leased to Jacob A. Wright, later owner of the Franklin Hotel in Hagerstown, Maryland.[17] Governor Bigler of Pennsylvania was wined and dined at Buena Vista on July 4, 1852.[18] By this time, the Inn had under gone many changes of name: Maguire's, to Maguire's Place, to Cold Springs, to Beautiful View, to Buena Vista Springs, to Buena Vista Springs Hotel.[19]

The management of the old lodging changed just about as often as its name. In 1856, Daniel and Elizabeth Dysert were lessees.[20] In 1858, Aaron Beck tried his hand at being host.[21]

---

16 *Franklin County Deed Book,* Vol. 21, July 22, 1847, p. 10.
17 *Village Record,* Waynesboro, Pa., June 2, 1852.
18 Ibid, July 1, 1852.
19 Ibid, May 22, 1856.
20 Ibid, May 22, 1856.
21 Ibid, April 7, 1858.

Mrs. Ann Cecilia Funk invested in a management interest in the watering place. Her son, David H. Funk, was the proprietor.[22] With so many changes in management, the upkeep on the property was poor and the buildings began to deteriorate.

It might be well to recount the traditions connected with the naming of Buena Vista and Monterey Springs. It should be remembered that the Mexican War (1846-48), over the annexation of Texas and other border disputes, occurred during the formative years of these old taverns and wagon stands as vacation resorts. Names of towns and sites where the U.S. Army engaged in battle during this war became "names in the news." These names were repeated, not only locally, but throughout the country. They were often used by soldiers who had served during the dispute because they were both distinct and popular. B.L. Maurer, Esq. stated in the *Kittochtinny, Historical Papers*, Vol. II, page 310, February 21, 1900:

> "That (Monterey Springs) had no name of special significance until after the Mexican War...when a large brick building was given the name of Monterey after a city of that name captured by General Taylor during the Mexican War."

Another legend has it that Madame Don Augustine de Iturbide, Empress of Mexico, 1822-23, (widow of the extravagant and arbitrary emperor, deposed and executed in 1824), fled Mexico for Philadelphia, passed this way and stayed at Ripple's Inn at the mountaintop. Because the summit, rimmed in by mountains, was a reminder of her native

---

22 Ibid, April 7, 1859.

Monterey in Mexico, she called it *Monterey*. Then, too, from the veranda at Maguire's Cold Springs, upon seeing the landscape of unending ridges, she was heard to say in her native language "Buena Vista" meaning "a Beautiful View." Unfortunately, we have nothing to substantiate either circumstance.

Madam Iturbide lived and died in Philadelphia. Her children attended the seminaries at Emmitsburg in Maryland. She probably was a frequent visitor to the area while her children were in school.

These names gave a certain illustrious distinction to the resorts which no longer exist. Whatever their origin, the Spanish names today remain, although the pronunciation of Buena Vista has been regionalized to "Beeuna Vista" or "Bona Vista." Pronunciation of Monterey has remained Monterey. Since that time, at least, five major wars have come and gone, the celebrated hotels and their guests have come and gone, only the names remain.

One of these wars, the Civil War, had begun in 1861. If Maryland was a border state, then the summit of the South Mountain was a border area. The hotels of the mountain were:

> resorted to in times of rebel invasion by, not only many persons of Washington and Antrim Townships of this county (Franklin County, PA.) but many from Washington County, Maryland and the Valley of Virginia. At this place, (Monterey) in times of danger, pickets were always placed from Monterey House to the westward side of the mountain (Buena Vista) to give notice if the rebles (sic) were approaching.[23]

---

23 David Miller, Jr., Letter to the *Valley Spirit,* Chambersburg, PA. Issue- Dec 15, 1886.

Buena Vista Springs Inns and Bath Houses

An artist's conception, taken from *McCauley's History of Franklin County of 1876* of the original Maguire establishments, after the improvements of Valentine B. Gilbert. These buildings stood along Old Rt. 16, near the intersection of the Buena Vista Road. Large Buena Vista Springs Hotel, was built in 1891, top center, at the skyline.

Photo-Courtesy of Kenton H. Broyles

Buena Vista Inn - 1900

This building had been built in the early 1840's by John Maguire as an adjunct to his "wagon tavern." which was to the left in the above photo. It was remodeled many times operated as a boarding house, in the 1920's. The building was razed in 1943.

Signal fires were kept laid to notify those in the valley below, that it was time to "skedaddle" to the covert of the mountain with their livestock and valuables. A local newspaper offered after the Battle of Gettysburg:

> *A variety of rumors have been circulating here to the effect, that the Rebels have invaded Maryland again, all of which have proven unfounded. It would be well for farmers and others having stock to be in readiness in case of invasion or raid.*[24]

The Monterey Pass, as it came to be called in the official dispatches of both armies, found itself in the line of advance and retreat from the Battle of Gettysburg. After the retreat from Gettysburg, pickets continued their watch along the peaks.

> *One night last week, a soldier from this place was shot at near Buena Vista Springs, while out on picket duty, the ball passing close to his head.*[25]

After the war ended, Ann C. Funk and James Hovis were the lessees of Buena Vista Springs. Advertisements offered, "table, bar and stabling." The old Inn was being featured as a restaurant. During the post-war depression of 1866-67, the property was repeatedly offered for sale. The last offering in 1867 stated, "for rent, if not sold this time!"

Valentine B. Gilbert, son of John Gilbert from Waynesboro, sought to retire to a gentleman's life. He had been a successful farmer, orchardist and businessman. On April 1, 1865 he had bought the Waynesboro Hotel, where the First National Bank

---

24 *Village Record*, Waynesboro, Pa., September 11, 1863.
25 "A Soldier Shot At," *Village Record*, Waynesboro, Pa. September 18, 1863.

now stands, from Francis Bowden. The bustling town life probably did not suit him; so he sold the hotel exactly two years after he had bought it.[26] Mr. Gilbert bought the Buena Vista Springs property with the intention of remodeling the old mansion into summer home for his retirement.[27] Remodel it he did; retire he did not! He cleared up the brush covered fields and planted them with orchards and extensive vineyards. He also renovated the mansion and hotel buildings, and improved the park and bath house across the turnpike. In general he gave the Buena Vista Springs Inn a new lease on life![27]

In the meantime, at the summit of the mountain, in the plateau east of the turnpike tollgate, changes were being made. This area, too, was turning into a resort. David Miller, Sr. (1797- 1870) purchased land from Henry Gordon's widow, where he started a new hotel building. This was 100 acres of Gordon farmland which had originally been part of a patent called "Bear Swamp" granted to Dr. Robert Johnston in 1782, in the right of Robert Cunningham. "Bear Swamp" encompassed all of what is now the Monterey Circle development, the Monterey Golf Course and Happel's Flat or Meadow as far west as the intersection of Old and New Routes 16.[28]

Dr. Johnston was a surgeon in the Revolution. Born in Washington Township, he served under Anthony Wayne at

---

26 *Franklin Co. Deed Books,* Vol. 42, p. 264, April 1, 1865, Vol. 42, p. 266, April 1, 1867, Vol. 42, p. 433, May 27, 1867.

27 I.H. McCauley, *Historical Sketch of Franklin County,* John M. Pomerey, D. F. Pursel, 1878, Chambersburg, Pa., Appendix p. 250.

28 *Franklin County Deed Book,* Vol. 44, p. 334, June 6, 1868 See Also *Franklin County Deed Book,* Vol. 4, p. 463; Aug. 1, 1799 & Land Patent, Books #1, p. 231; May 6, 1782 (PHMC).

Saratoga and became a personal friend of General Washington.

In fact, Washington visited him on his farm, south of Greencastle, during the Whiskey Rebellion of 1794. Dr. Johnston had been appointed Inspector of Excise for this region of Pennsylvania.[29]

We have two theories why Dr. Johnston would trouble himself with a small tract of land like "Bear Swamp," (188 ½ acres) when he owned much larger holdings of 1500 acres in Pennsylvania and over 5000 acres in the Kentucky Territory. First, Johnston was probably aware of the studies by Dr. Benjamin Rush of Philadelphia dealing with the healing powers of mineral spring water in Pennsylvania. Rush's studies were written in 1776 and Johnston's friend, George Washington, was a proponent of mineral baths. Washington visited the mineral baths of Bath, Virginia, now Berkeley Springs, West Virginia. Johnston received title to the "Bear Swamp" on May 6, 1782 and applied for a license to keep a public house of entertainment on July 25, 1782. Perhaps Dr. Johnston opened or planned to open the first mineral spa on our mountain top!

Secondly, in 1784, Johnston travelled to China as one of this country's first Foreign Ministers, in an effort to open trade relations with that country. On his travels to China, he took with him quantities of *ginseng* (Panax Cinquefolium) or *manroot* which at that time was worth its weight in gold. Possibly he reaped a crop of this prized herb from the swamp on our mountaintop. When he returned he was a wealthy man.

---

29 John M. Palmer, *Kittochtinny Historical Papers,* Vol. 13, p. 214, Chambersburg, Pa., 1953.

He settled near Greencastle where he died in 1808, leaving a large estate. He had disposed of the "Bear Swamp" tract to Patrick Mooney in 1798, who bought it for his son, William Mooney. The two of them kept a store and tavern along the Baltimore Road known today as Monterey.[30]

In 1798, this tract was improved by a one story 38 x 18 foot round log dwelling with three windows in good shape, a log stable 30 x 15 feet, and a frame shade (shed) 52 x 12 feet.[31] This was a sizable installation for this time, but, the traffic through the gap to and from York, Philadelphia and Baltimore was considerable. In 1819, William Mooney sold his tavern and storeroom to Lewis Ripple, Sr., a neighbor and wagoner, who had, taken up the Rocky Spring tract, in 1784, where he had a wagonstand. This tract surrounded the crossroads today of Old and New Routes 16 and bounded the "Devils Race Course" on the East.[32]

Here we might interpose a description of the Mt. Zero area, since it centered in and around Lewis Ripple's tract of land and first wagonstand. Mt. Zero or Zero, as it was called, was the center point of three cross roads, these being: the Waynesburg, Green-castle, Mercersburg Turnpike, the Chambersburg to Baltimore road, and the old Furnace Road (Fairfield Road). The turnpike tollgate house still stands having been established in 1828.[33] It is thought that the little brick schoolhouse located

---

30 *Franklin County Deed Book*, Vol. 4, p. 344, Sept. 6, 1798.
31 *U.S. Direct Tax of 1798*, On Microfilm #372, Tax List for Penna., National Archives, 1963, p. 832.
32 State Land Office, *Patent Books*.
33 *Franklin County Deed Book*, Vol. 15, p. 497, Mar. 3, 1828. PHMC.

west of the tollgate house was established about 1839. The last Zero schoolhouse still stands on the hill overlooking the tollgate. This served as a school until 1892.

There was also an official post office at Zero from February 7, 1837 until April 10, 1839. Lewis Ripple was the first postmaster, John P. Baker was the second and last postmaster. For over thirty-two years after its closing Zero was an *unofficial* post office. The mail stage would drop the mail at the tollgate or tavern and it would be gratuitously delivered.[34] The origin and meaning of Zero or Mt. Zero seems lost, as we have found no documentation for its genesis. This may have been the zero mile measurement point for Lewis Ripple's wagon business, or, as others claim, for the winter temperatures which were often read at the tollgate.

Lewis Ripple's first wagon stand stood near the entrance to Rolando Woods Park of the Blue Ridge Summit Lions Club, along present Charmian Road. These buildings were constructed about 1810 and were destroyed by fire a few years thereafter. He immediately rebuilt a roomy stone structure on the same site. This came to be called Ripples Tavern and also, was completely destroyed by fire in 1817.[35] Following this, Ripple bought the Mooney establishment, as mentioned, on August 18, 1819. He removed the old log tavern and replaced it with a larger frame one. It was this tavern that came to be known as "Monterey House."

Ripple continued his freighting to Baltimore and Pittsburgh, and continued to operate the popular watering place until the

---

34 U. L. Gordy, *Kittochtinny Historical Papers*, Vol. 11, p. 555, Chambersburg, Pa., 1938.

35 *Record Herald*, Waynesboro, Pa., July 7, 1942.

spring of 1846, when he sold it to another neighbor, Samuel Buhrman.

Mr. Buhrman (1812-1861) was born near Mt. Zion, Frederick County, Maryland and had engaged in farming there and on the Monterey property of his father-in-law, Henry Gordon. The Monterey House was completely renovated and had built a rapidly increasing clientele. Disastrously, it was destroyed by fire in February 1849.

In 1850, Buhrman reconstructed this building which was 90 feet long, and erected a new modern brick structure which was more roomy, luxurious, and serviceable. He styled (named) it the Monterey Springs Hotel.[36] It was under his tenure that Monterey made its transition from an unsophisticated wagon tavern to a fashionable health and vacation resort.

Much advertising proclaimed the remarkable salubrity of the mountain air and the purity of the waters as a remedy, if not a cure. The elevation "above the Vapors" gave exemption from malaria, was especially good for lung and throat troubles, and general debility. The waters were acclaimed for irregularity, summer complaint, and female troubles. An article in the *Village Record*, Waynesboro, Pa. of June 30, 1853 offered:

> *About this time, with the thermometer ranging from 96-100 in the shade, folks begin to feel like enjoying the realities of "mountain life." The different watering places on the South Mountain, all delightful places of resort, are now open for the reception of visitors and not a few, of late, have been moving in that direction.*

---

36 Ibid, Issue A, July 7, 1942, Waynesboro, Pa.

Ripple-Buhrman Tavern About 1920
"Monterey House"

This old building pre-dated 1850. It stood near the intersection of present day Monterey Avenue and Charmian Road, on the site of the present golf course. It was used variously as a store, a tavern and a wagon-stand. It was moved to the east side of Monterey Avenue, present Joseph Bradley, where it became a rental cottage. This was the famous "Square Cottage' where Wallis Warfield was born June 19th, 1896; when her parents vacationed there. She returned once to Monterey and Blue Ridge Summit to visit relatives when she was ten years old. The Square Cottage was gutted by fire on July 2, 1942 and was torn down with other larger buildings.

The springs had always been a seasonal business, whether for reasons of health or finance. Samuel Buhrman leased the management of Monterey Springs to William B. Rodgers, of Baltimore. Rodgers seemed determined to upgrade the hotel and make it a successful enterprise. On June 23, 1856, Monterey Springs opened with a Grand Ball. Both the Hagerstown and Waynesboro Brass Bands were present for the occasion, attracting a large crowd.[37] Mr. Rodger's first season attracted over one hundred regular guests. In August of 1857, the following year, seventy regular boarders were present, increasing to eighty toward September 1st.[38]

In the *Village Record*, Waynesboro, Pa. issue of March 25, 1858, Mr. Rodgers advertised:

For the Coming Season
Monterey Springs

The undersigned having leased the above well known "Hotel and Watering Place" situated on the top of South Mountain, is preparing to accommodate the traveling public. Having made and intending to make many more improvements that will conduce to the comfort of his guests, he hopes to merit liberal patronage. His Table will be provided with the best the market affords, his Bar, the choicest liquors and his Stables, at all times, attended by careful Hostlers.

William B. Rodgers

Hiring out a livery for a drive, to see the sights or to visit friends and picnic was becoming the vogue. Whist and social dancing were becoming stylish, along with changes in dress

---

37 *Village Record*, Waynesboro, Pa., Issue 23, June 1856.
38 Ibid, Issue 6, August 1857.

and customs. Bare arms and low necked dresses were the fashion. We note, again from the *Village Record,* August 18, 1859, in the letter of a young servant to her family:

> *"as for low-necked dresses, the lower it is, the more fashionable you are, and the less clothes you wear the more fashionable you are dressed—Miss Julia gave me a blue silk dress of hers and I cut its neck off and Susie Simmons cut the neck off hers and we attracted so much attention to our necks, promenading in the street like the other ladies and holding up her clothes and the higher you hold them, the more you are thought of."*

Finding that the profits could not cover his debts on the lease and the improvements he had made, Mr. Rodgers relinquished his lease to Monterey Springs, in 1860.

Samuel Buhrman died February 14, 1861. His heirs and administrators leased the premises to David Miller, Sr. (1797-1870). Mr. Miller was a native of Lebanon County and had lived in Waynesboro, and Washington County, Maryland. He was a genteel and knowledgeable host and evidently an experienced innkeeper. His hospitality was highly regarded, but, it was of a more erudite nature than those of his predecessors. The Miller operation was a family affair. He ran the Monterey Springs with his son David as farmer, and his three sisters, Misses Sarah and Caroline Miller and widow Catherine Miller Waddell, as housekeepers and cooks.[39] Miller operated the Monterey Springs Hotel from April, 1861 until April 1866, through the years of the Civil War. During the time of the

Monterey Springs Hotel 1875

This view shows the Monterey House Complex almost from the beginning. It stood at the SE intersection of Monterey Avenue and and the old Turnpike, present Charmian Road, opposite the golf course. The square and attached long building far right, were the original Ripple and Buhrman Tavern respectively.

Monterey Inn 1920

This tranquil snow scene shows the Monterey Inn of the V. E. Holmes 1870's era. The annex (orig. Monterey Springs Hotel); Square Cottage (Ripple's Tavern); Long Cottage (Buhrman's) and Monterey "House." The buildings, (right in photo) were moved from the opposite (West) side of Monterey Avenue, in 1850, later moved again, in 1874, to make room for the Monterey Springs Hotel (left).

Confederate retreat from the Battle of Gettysburg, he and everyone in the old hotel were placed under house arrest and confined inside. Only his son, David, and his nephew, William Waddell were allowed about to tend the livestock and perform the outside farm chores.[40]

Generals Judson Kilpatrick and the "Boy General," George Armstrong Custer consulted for a time at the Monterey Springs Hotel that dark and stormy night of July 4-5, 1863.[41] It is doubtful that any officers of either Army tarried long at Monterey, although later advertising and literature claims that almost all the "big" military names were entertained either at Monterey Springs or the Clermont, even though the Clermont had not yet been built!!

David Miller left Monterey Springs in the spring of 1866. He began construction of the Clermont House on the hundred acres he had purchased from the Henry Gordon Estate.

Clermont House was a three and one-half story frame building, with an observatory on top. It commanded a spectacular view of the Gettysburg Valley. With accommodations for 125 persons, the house had ample porches on three floors, and a large veranda on the first floor which was added at a later date. It had a large parlor, library, office, dining room which seated 125 persons, large kitchen, spacious halls, fifty-two bedrooms; consisting of 40 doubles and 12 single rooms, five

---

39 I.H. McCauley, *Historical Sketch of Franklin County*, John F. Pomeroy and D.F. Pursel, 1878, Chambersburg, Pa. Appendix p. 257.
40 Letter of David Miller, Jr. to Valley Spirit, Chambersburg, Pa., Issue 15, Dec. 1886
41 Op. Cit.

master bathrooms and 19 toilets. Out-buildings consisted of a servants building of 16 rooms, an eight room owners cottage and a stable. A deep well and steam water pump completed the complex.[42]

It is possible that David Miller, Sr. chose to leave Monterey Springs Hotel because of water problems, since his successors in ownership seem to have struggled long and hard with this problem. In spite of all the publicity and good health hyperbole that was printed and passed along over the years regarding the hygenic springs at Monterey, this installation was always lacking a flowing mountain spring, with the exception of Rocky Spring, one-half mile west from Monterey along the turnpike.

In 1876, Persifor Frazer, Jr., a field geologist with the Second Geological Survey of Pennsylvania, while investigating the temperature of different springs in relation to the strata from which they issued, stated:

> *Notes on some Springs:*—Near Monterey (Franklin County) The ridges of the South Mountain in the neighborhood of Monterey furnish abundant springs, though there is none on the site known as the Monterey Springs Hotel. The latter is supplied by a pump which never runs dry.

According to this same report, there was a well in the cellar of the Monterey Springs Hotel. Another pump and well fronted the house but was separated from it by the road. A third pump was situated in the stable yard to the north of the hotel.[43]

---

42 *Sale Bill*, Mrs. Charles Cowman, 18, Aug. 1936 np. nd.

The fact that Rockey or Brown's Spring presented problems to the Buhrman's is obvious. Whether due to considerable reduction in the flow of water or whatever the problem, Buhrman's heirs disposed of the Rocky Spring tract and surrounding land to John Wesley Brown in 1864. They later bought a two and one-half acre tract with a cold spring about three-fourths of a mile east of the Monterey Hotel at a sharp curve in the turnpike. It is here, on the property now owned by Stanley Dingle, that Buhrman's heirs erected bath houses.[44]

Henry Yingling purchased the Monterey Springs Hotel in June of 1866 when David Miller left his lease. Yingling improved the baths at Monterey, but could not make a success of the business. He was in and out of receivership twice during the thirteen years that he ran the hotel.[45] Perhaps, David Miller's new hostelry had drawn away the bulk of the boarders. In addition the Gettysburg Battlefield was becoming an attraction and many new hotels were opening.[46] One of these located on the hill north of Monterey was the Montana Springs resort. There was also another vacation area springing up along the turnpike at Fountaindale, midway between Emmitsburg and Monterey Springs. Mr. Fred McIntire featured pure mountain air, cool spring water, plenty of ice and bath house and sumptuous fare.[47]

---

43 Persifor Frazer, Jr., *Second Geological Survey Of Penna.*, Vol. CCC, p. 249 & 347, Harrisburg, Pa. 1880.

44 *Franklin County Deed Book*, Vol. 38. p. 434, 1864; *Franklin County Deed Book*, Vol. 63, p. 290, Sept. 30, 1879.

45 *Franklin County Deed Book*, Vol. 44, p. 65, June 22, 1866.

46 George R. Webb, *Jaunts, Illustrated*, Western Md. Railway American Banknote Co. Press, np.; nd.

The Clermont was opened for business in July, 1868 by David Miller, Sr. His lordship of the manor was brief, he died in 1870. The summer hotel continued under the management of his son, David, a graduate of Franklin and Marshall College. Over the years he built up a distinguished clientele of artists, writers, clergyman, barristers and military officers. It was a quiet haven for the creative and the learned.[48]

I offer here an excerpt from a booklet entitled *Clermont Monterey 1871-1904* written by Edward L. Keys, the son of a famous Boston surgeon and a gentlemen's gentleman. Mr. Keys, who claimed to be a writer and poet, lived at various hotels and boarding houses at Blue Ridge Summit. In later years, Keys made his home at Charmian and eventually died there. This excerpt gives a first hand view of travel and vacationing at our mountain resorts in the days before the railroad. Edward Keys begins:

> Those who remember the month of May, 1871 may recall how Baltimoreians scattered early from the hot bricks and cobblestones of the city. I joined in the flight, escaping so far as Mechanicstown (now Thurmont), which was then the terminus of the Western Maryland R.R. The road was completed in the summer of 1872.
>
> Though it was early morning when I left the city, yet it was quite noon when this point was reached. The slow, rough tiresome ride left me hungry; and Emmitsburg (seven miles distant) was the nearest place to get anything to eat.
>
> I chartered a vehicle resembling a condemned ambulance and which was propelled by a blind, spavined horse and was "hauled" to the quaint old Maryland town.

---

47 *Village Record*, Waynesboro, Pa., Issue 19 June 1868; Issue 12 March 1874.
48 Ibid, Issue 12 March 1874.

Here I fared very well. Greatly refreshed, I decided to continue my journey. After some trouble, I managed to secure a debilitated hack, which, a century earlier, had probably seen service in some city, and started for the "top of the mountain."

The driver was a fresh and strange type. His figure "favored" an elongated hairpin. His scanty apparel was shapeless and colorless—like a dirty fog; but his headpiece interested me immensely. The body was of brown corduroy; extending brim was of thick leather with a patent leather finish. A Texan cowboy would have given a fortune or gladly violated all the commandments, to possess such a maverick sombrero just for an hour.

I rode with him on the box, enjoying my pipe and the magnificent mountain scenery, but his vocal battery compelled me to retreat within.

"What trade do yer foller?"

"Is Bostin bigger than Gettsburg?"

"Why didn't they make a parson of yer?"

"Parsons have good pickin an are sure of chicken wherever they go!"

Thus I was vanquished.

His neck, which had the length and elasticity of a giraffe's anticipated the modern "rubber-neck"; for when he passed Fountaindale, his unique face was twisted down to the window and he shrieked:

"That's Claremont up on the knob."

In the distance, I was able to see an isolated barren structure. I shall never forget how this same structure impressed me when an hour later we drove through the gateway—into a space which was an admirable lawn, decorated by what struck me to be an abandoned barrack.

That it wasn't and old building was apparent, for it was guiltless of its first coat of paint and it looked so homely, so ungainly. Not a human being, nor a beast were in sight.

After an interval, the proprietor appeared, sauntering down

the piazza toward us. His mouth holding a twig, which he was eating, and his hand carrying a hoop-pole, serving for a cane.

He greeted the driver warmly, who was clearly a personage of local prominence and who reciprocated the civility cheerfully. He informed me then that he "hadn't looked for me before tomorrow." I disembarked and was shown my room—Northwest exposure, first floor. It was about 10 by 12 feet carpetless and cell-like. The little mirror fastened to the wall suggested a piece of polished corrugated tin, and the table, formed by the co-partnership of a barrel and a board, showed unmistakably that the primitiveness was the motto of the ranch.

In lieu of a chair, I threw myself upon the bed; the contact was painful, the couch was harder than my luck. An hour later, I discovered that no pains were taken to conceal that the guests comprised three spinsters whose united ages summed up to two hundred and thirty-four years.

The next morning I turned out early—I was tired. Getting up might rest me. I went out on the porch and looked off its east end—there was no eastern porch as there is now.

"What a superb view!" I involuntarily exclaimed; "this delicious air is more bracing than a brandy and soda." The grandeur of the scenery and the wilderness of the surrounding country were impressive. Excepting the residence of Mr. Gladhill, far to the northward and few yet standing low in the vale, not a building could be seen. If I am not mistaken, there were but four houses "on the pike" between Clermont and Fountaindale.

This early morning proved to be more than of sufficient (reward) to banish the shock of yesterday.[49]

This was the Clermont-Monterey area, still in its pristine provinciality. There had been a post-office recently established at the Monterey Springs Hotel after a lapse in mail service of 32

---

49 Edward L. Keys, Pamphlet, *Clermont-Monterey 1871-1904*, np.; nd.; pp 3-6.

Clermont House - 1876

This rendering of Clermont from McCauley's History of Franklin County; 1876. It was a stately 3½ story frame building with 52 bedrooms, a dining room that seated 125 persons, a 16 room servants quarters, an 8 room residence and a barn and stable.

Photo-Courtesy of Kenton H. Broyles

Clermont House - 1920

The veranda facing the Gettysburg Valley is evident in this snow scene, it was not original, but a later addition. The owner's dwelling, can be seen through the trees, far right in photo. This refined hostelry operated into the 1930's. It was torn down, albeit in fine condition in 1940.

years. Harry Yingling was the postmaster.⁵⁰ The only sort of mass transportation to this section was the Hagerstown-Gettysburg Stage," which passed through this area every other day.

Everyone was clamoring for a railroad ever since the bankruptcy, abandonment or failure of Thaddeus Stevens infamous "Tapeworm" railway. This erratic state railroad had ended its meanderings right here on this mountaintop in 1839, and the need for some sort of better transportation was felt. To drive a wagon or herd to Baltimore and make the return trip took approximately five days. There had been promise upon promise of a railroad for more than a quarter of a century. The stalemates were mostly financial.

The Gettysburg Railroad had been trying to raise money for an extension to Waynesboro and Hagerstown for years without success. The Northern Central Railroad wanted to connect to Baltimore but not Waynesboro. The Cumberland Valley Railroad had bought the defunct Franklin Railroad so it could connect southward to the B and O Railroad. The Western Maryland Railroad under the leadership of John Lee Chapman had laid iron as far as Sabillasville on August 28, 1871. This thwarted the act of Pennsylvania Legislature passed in 1866. This act allowed the Gettysburg Railroad preferential use of the Western Maryland line if it entered Pennsylvania.⁵¹

Mr. Chapman was instrumental in getting both the Cities of Baltimore and Hagerstown to subscribe bonds for the connection of the railway between Sabillasville and Hagerstown.

50 U.L. Gordy, *Kittochtinny Historical Papers,* Vol. 11, p. 555 Chambersburg, Pa., 1938.
51 *Village Record,* Waynesboro, Pa., May 19, 1865; Sept. 21, 1866; Aug. 16, 1872, Aug. 6, 1879; passim.

Charging graft and mismanagement this extension was hotly opposed because of the cost, even though both cities badly needed the trade.[52]

Now the dilemma! There were three routes proposed by engineers for the Western Maryland Railroad to extend its line into Pennsylvania, which would lengthen the line and raise cost tariff. One route was to swing the line south of the mountain going by Mt. Zion and Buzzard's Knob, but the high cost of excavation and the hard terrain rendered this route unfeasible. Another was to drive a tunnel three thousand feet long, through the hard copper rock at the summit of the Blue Ridge.

John Lee Chapman, however, was a man of great influence. If he could not raise the money for the project, he had friends that could. So to avoid the expensive Maryland routes and the costly lengthening of the road into Pennsylvania, he personally bought two farms at, as he called it, the "Blue Ridge or Monterey Summit." Both farms bounded the Mason-Dixon Line. The farm in Maryland, which is now the Roland Hill Development, he bought from David W. Willard. The farm on the Pennsylvania side of the line, the former D.F. Benchoff farm, he bought from Augustus M. Price.[53]

It was easy! "Put the roadbed where you will," said Mr. Chapman to his engineers. The rail line swung around the mountain a short distance into Pennsylvania, thus avoiding the

---

52 Ibid, Aug. 31, 1866.
53 *Franklin County Deed Book,* Vol. 48, 138, 141, Aug. 9, 1870; Vol. 50, p. 302 Apr. 1, 1872.

tunnel. Although it wasn't as easy as it sounded! From Sabillasville to the summit, deep rock cuts were needed, and these were days before dynamite was in common use. In April of 1872, a heavy rock slide blocked the road for several days. But, the summit of the Blue Ridge had been reached, Blue Ridge Summit had been born![54]

At Pen Mar, two and one-half miles further west, the same problem of entering Pennsylvania was encountered. Essentially the same act was played again, this time with different thespians. The line swung into Pennsylvania on private land once again without a corporate charter. The railroad was opened on August 3, 1872.[55]

The Summit or highest point on the railroad is at or near the crossing of the tracks with Monterey Road, about 1400 feet above sea level. During the April Term of Franklin County Quarter Sessions in 1852, the road to Monterey was ordered to be built as a public road beginning at Buhrman's Tavern at the Baltimore Turnpike in order to connect with the public roads leading to Sabillasville and to Middletown Valley as far as the Maryland Line.[56]

In 1872, at the time the railroad was built, the Sabillasville Road was relocated to run parallel to the railroad track, as it does now, and to pass under trestling where the concrete underpass is now. The present crossing at the Summit station has remained essentially the same.[57]

---

54 Harold A. Williams, *Western Maryland Railway Story*, WMRR Baltimore, Md., 1952, p. 54.
55 Ibid, p. 55.
56 Franklin County Clerk of Courts, *Road Docket 1849-1863*, p. 76.

John Lee Chapman had reserved the right to build a station and warehouse on his land, so as to derive rent from the railroads for these buildings. Surplus farm and woodland presented a problem. For several seasons, Mr. Chapman lived in the Willard farmhouse. He erected a steam sawmill. Here the lumber was sawn to build the first railroad station and warehouse. This warehouse stood where O.E. Weikert's former garage building stands and the first station was erected directly across the tracks on the North side near the present signal block. Fronting on the railroad and the road leading to it, west of Monterey Lane, was a pasture and grove of trees which Chapman decided to develop as a picnic area.[58] On this tract containing about twenty-five acres, he erected, in 1874, a pavilion 42 by 87 feet. A twelve foot wide porch extended across the front or North side.

The Village Record of September 10, 1874 stated:

> The Pavillion (sic) recently erected at the Blue Ridge Station on the W.M.R.R. by the Hon. J.L. Chapman, was opened with a pic-nic on Monday last and ended with a cotillion party in the evening. The attendance we learn was large, persons being present from Baltimore, Westminster, Emmitsburg, Hagerstown and other points along the line of the road. The Band of the 6th Maryland Regiment was in attendance and the music furnished is represented as having been grand.

The Park and Pavilion proved to be so popular, that Chapman decided to further develop the grove of trees as a

---

57 Harold A. Williams, *Western Md. Railway Story*, Baltimore 1952, p. 131.
58 *Franklin County Will Book*, Vol. "I" p.475, March 30, 1876.

First Blue Ridge Summit Station WMRR
1884 Photo

This station was built by John Lee Chapman in 1872 and leased to the WMRR along with the warehouses across the tracks. The depot stood on the north side of the present tracks, opposite the existing signal block. Chapman's Pavilion stood north and west of the station across Dutrow Avenue.

Chapman's Pavilion 1884

This group, apparent "hikers" with snake sticks in hand was only one of the many groups that sought comfort and comradery at the popular pavilion. Imagine the patience it must have taken to pose this group. Those seated are on newspaper "Sunday clothes" were hard come by in those days. Pavilion was 42' by 87'; porch 12' wide on side opposite in photo. Lumber for its construction was sawn on the site.

campground. He erected an observatory, similar to those later erected at Pen Mar, on the hill in Maryland, near the present water reservoir. This overlooked the Park and the valley below. Hiking was a popular pastime. Livery business, on the site, was managed by Chapman's son-in-law, Charles C. Dutrow. The grove became a place of comfort for railroad excursionists, as well as, a community center for farmers and local residents. Before there were any churches at the Summit (1884), Martin Hawley held the first Sunday School in the Pavilion. Church services came to be held regularly, along with revival services, reunions, and dances.[59]

Chapman built two cottages along the road to the depot. One was at the corner of Monterey Lane and the Depot Road, (present Dutrow Avenue) now known as "Summit Villa." The other, several hundred feet west on Depot Road, (Dutrow Avenue) toward Flohr Lumber Company, was originally frame, but, is now encased in brick. These cottages rented well, but were of small capacity. Hence, the two-story stone *Mountain House* was built opposite them, across the tracks, adjoining Chapman's warehouse. A third story was added later. *Mountain House* was operated by his wife and his daughter, Margaret Lee Chapman McComas.[60]

Further west along the tracks, David Willard opened *The Willard Springs Hotel* at approximately the same time as the Mountain House opened.[61]

John Lee Chapman was born on February 18, 1812 of

---

59 *Record Herald*, Waynesboro, Pa., July 5, 1929, p. 19 and 20.
60 *Franklin County Will Book*, "I," p. 475, Mar. 30, 1876, *OCD* "T," p. 295.

Chapman Manor About 1912

This building still exists between the Old Station Library, Maryland-Midland RR and the Mason-Dixon line. It is now called the Summit Hill Apartments and is a rental dwelling. It has had a varied career as the Chapman residence, a hotel, a rooming house for soldiers during WWII and as the Hiram Hotel in the post-war years it was a hostelry with bar and dining facilities.

Scotch lineage. He was a successful drug merchant and glass manufacturer. He was Mayor of Baltimore 1861–1867, President of the Western Maryland R.R. 1866–1868 and U.S. Naval Storekeeper, Port of Baltimore 1869–1873. He died November 18, 1880.[62]

If John Mifflin Hood was the father of Pen Mar, John Lee Chapman was the father of Blue Ridge Summit!

The Western Maryland Railway Company had almost concurrently established a park and pavilion like John Chapman's at Greenwood, nine miles from the station in Baltimore. The park had a pavilion, restaurant, lake for boating, swings, fountains and promenades. The company was already offering inducements for privately owned resorts in the Blue Ridge because they found that their passengers spurned Greenwood for the wild natural beauty of our mountains and wanted to travel further from home.[63]

Alexander Reiman, the former president of the railroad company and John Mifflin Hood, the new president whom Reiman had helped secure, opened Pen Mar Amusement Park on August 31, 1877. This park was three miles westward along the track toward Hagerstown from Blue Ridge Summit depot. In conjunction with this park, on March 28, 1883, a hotel corporation was formed called the *Blue Ridge Hotel Company*. Mr. Hood was probably seeking additional capital for the construction of the luxurious hotel when his special train "The

---

61 *Record Herald*, Waynesboro, Pa., July 5, 1930.
62 Vertical File, *Maryland Historical Society*, Baltimore, Md.
63 Harold A. Williams, *Western Maryland Railway Story*, WMRR, Baltimore, 1952, p. 83

Photo-Courtesy O.E. Weikert, Jr.

J.L. Chapman's "Mountain House"
Circa - 1920

Clearly this was the first hostelry at the "Summit." The frame end, left in photo, was opposite first depot and was built as a railroad warehouse, It was originally two stories, third story later added. It stood along south side of tracks on site of first Weikert Garage, now Church Street. Well foundation and stump of tree, at left still evident.

Chapman Cottage "Summit Villa"
Circa 1884

This building still stands, largely unaltered at the corner of Monterey Avenue and Depot Road (now Dutrow Avenue) and was one of two boarding houses built by J.L. Chapman. Monterey Ave. leading north toward Monterey can be seen at extreme right of photo.

Blue Mountain House" arrived at Pen Mar on May 29, 1883, bearing as his guests Francis T. King, Francis White, Dr. James Carey Thomas, Judge Fisher and others of Baltimore. They returned to Baltimore attached to the 4:06 pm train.[64] The Blue Mountain House opened that summer in 1883. $225,000 had been invested in the huge 200 room hotel which could house 1400 guests.[65]

At least two of his guests were members of the board of the Blue Ridge Hotel Company and were the first "summer people" in the Monterey-Clermont area. Francis T. King had bought the summer cottage of Dr. Herman J. Groesbeck, across the pike from the Clermont House in the spring of 1883. Dr. James Carey Thomas had built his summer residence called "Coombe Edge" along Monterey Lane, about halfway between what is now PA Rt. 16 and the Charmian Road.[66]

Dr. James Carey Thomas, at that time, was one of Baltimore's most prominent physicians. Francis T. King was a Baltimore financier, banker, friend and confidant of Johns Hopkins and directed the building of the hospital. Upon completion of the Western Maryland Railway to Hagerstown, Mr. King chartered the Monterey Land Company, Inc. whose land comprised nearly 300 acres surrounding the Monterey Inn, Monterey Circle and Golf Course and Monterey Peak properties. The original share holders in the Monterey Land Company were, in part, Francis T.

---

64 *Keystone Gazette,* Waynesboro, Pa., May 29, 1883.
65 Harold A. Williams, *Western Maryland Railway Story,* WMRR Baltimore, Md. 1952.
66 George L. Webb, *Jaunts, Illustrated,* Western Md. Railway American Banknote Co. Press, np.; nd.

Francis T. King's "Summer Cottage"
1st Summer Home at Monterey
Circa 1886

This frame residence has undergone many changes over the years, but it is still identifiable. It stands along the Charmian Road, opposite Greystone Inn and David Miller monument. It was either built or started by Dr. Herman Groesbeck of Baltimore, from whom King purchased it. F. T. King, was friend of Johns Hopkins and directed the building of the Hospital, he also chartered the Monterey Land Co.; which developed Monterey Inn and the Monterey Circle Area. Across the turnpike from this "cottage" was the Clermont House both properties commanded unsurpassed views of the Gettysburg Valley.

King, Francis White, John Curlett, James Carey, Sr. and Jr., Jesse Tyson, and Martin Hawley.[67]

From the first summer cottage of Dr. Groesbeck in 1873, expansion of the fashionable development was rapid. The Monterey Inn property was updated and improved by the Land Co. with special emphasis on the sewage and waterworks in preparation for future development. Some buildings were razed and others moved to new sites to conform to the lot plans and design of C.H. Latrobe, civil engineer of Baltimore. The brick Inn Building was enlarged with kitchen annex and dining room added. *Long Cottage,* the 90 foot frame building of Samuel Buhrman was modernized and moved further back from Monterey Lane.[68] *Square Cottage,* the *Buhrman's Tavern* of the 1850's, and later birthplace of Bessie Wallis Warfield Simpson, Duchess of Windsor, was refurbished into a rental cottage. The plans were grandiose, indeed, for this heretofore quiet hamlet, but, then, those who planned had the money to invest.

On April 5, 1876, the Monterey Springs Post Office was closed, and on that same day the Blue Ridge Summit Post Office opened under the same postmaster, Henry Yingling.[69]

At the other end of Monterey Lane, at the Summit, above the railroad, more philanthropic plans were being made. *Vacation Lodge,* a free rest hotel and vacation place for single, self-supporting working girls. The idea of a vacation hotel of nominal cost was conceived in the 1880's by Susan T. Murdoch,

---

67 Franklin County *Corporate Charters Docket,* April 29, 1874.
68 *Village Record,* Aug. 9, 1877.
69 U.L. Gordy, *Kittochtinny Historical Papers,* Vol. 11, p. 555 Chambersburg, Pa., 1938.

her sister, Mary Murdoch Norris and Mrs. Edward Davis. These three women united their efforts to solicit funds to support such a venture. In 1890, they leased the *Summit Villa* for two years, while continuing their efforts. In 1892, the *Vacation Lodge* was built.[70] It occupied the site of the present house of O.E. Weikert, Jr.

In 1889, the Baltimore and Harrisburg Company Division of the Western Maryland Railway was built from Highfield, Maryland to Fairfield, Pennsylvania, over most of the right-of-way of the Old Tapeworm or Pennsylvania State Railroad. This track crosses Route 16 just east of its intersection with Monterey Lane. Jack's Mountain was tunneled for about 450 feet through solid rock to make this connection. Laborers on this rail project were men of Irish, Italian, Hungarian, and Swedish immigrant stock. The tunnel was headed or broken through in March, 1889. Much credit is due to the immigrants who undertook this dangerous work, since cave-ins and rock slides were almost a daily occurrence. Main contractors on the job were Riley and Keough of Baltimore who employed local men as straw-bosses. Washington Benchoff and William E. Harbaugh, supervised gangs of men cutting the right-of-way free of timber and making cross-ties and laying iron.[71]

At the close of the building of the "Dutch Line" which was the local name given to this extension, because it was a connection into the Dutch country of Hanover and York. William Harbaugh was hired as a superintendent by the Buena Vista

---

70 *Record Herald,* Waynesboro, Pa., July 5, 1929, p. 20.
71 R.W. Harbaugh, *Record Herald,* July 5, 1929, p. 10.

Chapman's Tent Campground 1884 B.R.S

This picnic park, pavilion and campground was established by John Lee Chapman in 1874, prior to Pen Mar Park. It was on the north side of present Dutrow Ave. adjacent Flohr Lumber Co. It was a popular meeting place for worship, reunions, cotillions and conventions.

Vacation Lodge Built 1892 B.R.S.

This free, vacation rest home for single working girls was owned by the Cooperative Workers of the City of Baltimore. It occupied the site south of the railroad tracks opposite the present Blue Ridge Summit Free Library. (Old WMRR Station)

Photo Courtesy of Paul and Grace Mummert

Buena Vista Hotel
Circa - 1898

The new hotel sports its first coat of paint as the building's superintendent and crew pose, with his children, for the photograph in the early fall of 1898. Left to right in photo: Joe Eyler, rider; William E. Harbaugh (1868-1935) Superintendent; Edward Swisher, hands in pockets; Samuel Wetzel, beard; Harry V. Harbaugh, boy (b. 1893); Raymond W. Harbaugh, (b. 1897) babe-in-arms; George W. Socks, holding baby; James McClain, rider on the right. It appears that they have just closed the hotel for the season. The Post Office was under the veranda, door to far right in photo, at rear of horse.

Hotel Co. He worked for that company for more than forty years.

It was W.J.C. Jacobs who said that the first meeting between the principals of the Buena Vista Hotel Company and Valentine B. Gilbert took place close to the big rockery in Maguire's field, near the site where the hotel was eventually built.[72]

The Buena Vista Springs Improvement Company was formed on January 6, 1891 as a stock company of 900 shares of $100.00 each, $22,500 cash assets and the balance in land bought from Valentine B. Gilbert.[73] If the Blue Mountain House was so successful, why not capitalize on the same principle by building a grand hotel surrounded by a development of vacation houses founded on the beauties of nature and outdoor recreation? This grandiose layout would have everything, attract the best in clientele and be secluded from the maddening crowds of Pen Mar and the railroad excursionists.

Principals of the company were Mayor F.C. Latrobe of Baltimore; Robert Rennert, Baltimore hotelier; George K. McGaw, millionaire wholesaler of groceries and produce; and William S. Rayner, millionaire financier, shipping magnate and realtor, along with lesser millionaires like Joseph M. Cone, whose contracting firm did the construction work.[74]

The site selected was a rocky prominence on the mountain above V.B. Gilbert's Buena Vista Inn which was along the Baltimore Pike. One immediate problem with this site was that any road access was too steep to haul heavy building materials.

---

72 Ibid, p. 13.
73 Franklin County *Corporate Charters Docket,* January 6, 1891.
74 Ibid.

Immediately a railroad was laid from the Western Maryland at Germantown to the hotel site. A WMRR crew supervised by Mr. Harbaugh was sent to lay a railway line of standard gauge, lightweight rails to the hotel. This line was used to haul building materials to the site. A switch was cut into the main track of the Western Maryland and a boxcar pulled by horse teams to the hotel. However, the loads proved too heavy and time consuming. Whereupon several small flat-bottomed freight cars were purchased from the Washington, D.C. Street Railway Company and modified as flat cars to haul the freight. One was a large one with high sides, one was a small flat car, later used as a baggage wagon behind the open passenger-car. The Buena Vista Station on the Western Maryland was built largely at the expense of the hotel company. Passengers enjoyed the ride to and from the station in the picturesque horse drawn car. However, the original tracks had been laid close to the outside of the road, much to the-consternation of passengers who feared running off into the deep gorge that it paralleled. After the first season, the tracks were relaid to the inside of the right-of-way.[75]

The Buena Vista Springs Hotel was of Renaissance style and rose four stories on a solid rock foundation. The main building faced nearly due west with wings to the northwest, southwest, and south. The dining room was located in the southwest wing of the first floor. Kitchen facilities as well as the laundry occupied separate wings. The hotel had a frontage of 492 feet

---

75 R.W. Harbaugh, *Record Herald,* July 5, 1929, Waynesboro, Pa.

Buena Vista Horse Car About 1900

This classic photograph has been published repeatedly over the years. It was taken near the car-house site on Buena Vista Road, just south of the golf course. The guests delighted in the leisurely ride. The small flat baggage car was drawn by a pony or sometimes attached to the rear of the car. The car was reversed by hitching the horses to the opposite end!

Buena Vista Station WMRR 1912

This snapshot captures Blue Mt. Express on tracks and typical station life of the day. Girl, left hiking her stocking, baggage men at ready, passengers depart horse car and station for platform, girl in doorway, pinning her hat. Only thing missing is rowdy boys.

Buena Vista Springs Hotel Company Horsecar at Buena Vista Station
About 1900

This quaint, open-air horse-drawn streetcar carried guests and their luggage between the WMRR Station in Maryland and the grand hotel which was located about two miles north along what is now, (1982) Buena Vista Road. The atmosphere of the guests was always gay. They were on vacation and looking forward to a respite from the hum-drum life of the hot, humid, dull city sidewalks.

with a veranda fifteen feet wide running its entire length. On the first floor of the building were the lobby, offices, parlors, dining, sitting and reception rooms. The northwest and southwest wings contained sleeping quarters. There were suites with open fireplaces. Open fireplaces also embellished the parlors, sitting rooms, reading and writing rooms.[76]

Outdoor life featured hiking, promenading, horseback riding, tennis, and golf. Swimming was first tried in a pool near the bend in Old Route 16, near the Buena Vista Inn, but, the water was much too cold. It was later attempted to steam heat this pool without success. Finally the pool was filled in, and Lake Royer was featured for swimming and boating.

Although the peerless water supply was extolled at the hotel, there were problems with this from the start. The first season, the old Cold Spring failed. It was simply not adequate to supply a hotel of 180 rooms serving 400-500 people. The hotel contracted with the then failing Mont Alto Iron Company for a twenty-five acre tract of land on which there was a strong flowing spring at the headwaters of Mackey Run.[77] This spring necessitated laying a pipeline two miles in length and building an elevated wooden reservoir, which was destroyed in a forest fire in the 1920's.[78] A steam powered water pump was installed to augment the pressure in the top floors of the building. This Mackey Run spring is now part of the Washington Township Municipal Authority public water supply, and is located at the

---

[76] *Record Herald,* Waynesboro, Pa., July 5, 1929.
[77] *Franklin County Deed Books,* Vol. 90, p. 381, Nov. 11, 1891.
[78] *Record Herald,* Ibid.

Buena Vista Springs Swimming Pool
About 1910

This is a view of the Buena Vista Springs Hotel swimming pool and bathhouses. They were located in the bottom, north of the intersection of Buena Vista Road and Old Route 16, near the present pump house. They were located in an open park area replete with promenade, arbors, benches and gazebos. (See Illus. top p. 16)

head of the Run; east of the Mentzer Gap Road.

Because of its isolated location, this hotel was virtually self-sufficient in regard to its utilities. Its steam-power plant heated the building, pumped and heated the water, operated the laundry, lifted the elevator and ran the printing press. The hotel printed its own menus and brochures. It even pumped the gas for a unique low pressure gasoline vapor lighting system which was in use for many years, until wiring and a steam-powered electric generator were installed.

The golf course was originally six holes and kept mowed by a shepherd and his flock. It was later enlarged to nine holes and mowed with horse drawn mowers. Many dignitaries visited this hotel over the years and played this course.

Indoor life was not lacking, either. There were parlors and private banquet rooms, a barroom, billiard rooms, card and game rooms, bowling alleys, not to mention the Ballroom. On a still night one can almost hear the strains of the Lancers or a lilting waltz drifting on the mountain air, and see the ladies in their satin gowns and long gloves, checking their cards for the next dance and hear the fading sound of horse hooves on the gravel road, as laughter floats upward to the mountain top.[79]

This seems a long way from our starting point, and yet, not far at all. We have found our way back to Maguire's where the travelers once danced the rustic dances and jigs, and enjoyed life in as fine a style, with bowls of cider, minced pies, and roast goose, and vocal good cheer floating to the same

---

79 Pamphlet Vol. #1543, *Buena Vista Spring Hotel,* Unbound np.; nid.; Circa 1900, Penna. State Library, Harrisburg, Pa.

Buena Vista Springs Hotel About 1900

This photo taken from the Turnpike (Old Rt. 16) near present Capital Camps shows, not only the absence of timber on the mountainside, but, also, the first development houses built by George K. Magaw about 1899; far right, at the skyline.

Buena Vista Springs Hotel About 1920

This photo scales the size of the immense frame structure and its Renaissance style. A wing equal in length to the one, right center, extended eastward from the tower at far right. "The Seasons Observatory" and lobby entrance directly below it, at left. The dining room was on porch level near center of photo, dark windows.

mountain top?

The crude and rustic cabins that were our first resorts, the ordinaries, taverns and inns, the wagon and stage stops, the health resorts and hotels, the resplendent and refined resorts all have fallen to time and disappeared.

The Buena Vista Springs Hotel, the grandest of our Summit, closed its doors in 1931, but was in use as a reminder of a by-gone era until 1967, when it succumbed to fire. John Lee Chapman's Mountain House burned in 1935, his popular Pavilion and Park had long since been dismantled and disappeared. The Clermont House was razed in 1940 and Monterey Inn burned to the ground in 1943.

These were the beginnings and nucleus of the community of Blue Ridge Summit, that we know today.

Record Herald Photo

Ruins Of The Buena Vista Springs Hotel
December, 1967

This was the scene, toward dawn, December 8, 1967, a few hours after it was discovered the grand old hotel was ablaze. As the youngest of the Blue Ridge resorts it was the last to go. It had closed its doors as a hotel in 1931.

Colonial Counterfeiters
Of The Blue Ridge

(Part Two)

by
John Howard McClellan

Colonial Counterfeiters of the Blue Ridge

Part Two was originally presented
before the
Kittochtinny Historical Society
Chambersburg, Franklin County, Pennsylvania
November 17, 1988

Copyright © 1989 - John Howard McClellan

This edition was printed by
Copyquik Printing and Graphics, LLC
710 Oak Hill Avenue, Hagerstown, MD 21740

Manufactured in the United States of America

Library of Congress Cataloging Data

McClellan, John Howard, 1927-
   Colonial Counterfeiters of the Blue Ridge/John Howard McClellan
      p.   cm.
   Includes bibliographical references
   LC MLCM 92/08382 (F)
   1. Counterfeiters Pennsylvania
   2. Blue Ridge Counterfeiters—History

Cover sketch by Lester Jay Stone, 1976
printed with permission of the
Blue Ridge Summit Free Library, Blue Ridge Summit, PA 17214

Photographs herein are copyrighted to
John Howard McClellan, unless otherwise credited.
All Rights Reserved. 1989

Acknowledgements

After eight years of research into the subject matter of the following, it will come as no small surprise that the author came into contact with many people in the course of that research. It is only fitting that these individuals be thanked and acknowledged for the assistance they offered to me; many times voluntarily without being requested to do so.

Alexander Hamilton Free Library–Pam Coyle, Ruth Gembe, Diane Mellott
Blue Ridge Summit Free Library–Carol Bailey
Hamilton Library
Cumberland County Historical Society–Miriam Fox, Charles Hocking, Terry Koska, Linda Smith, Director
Ezra Lehman Library, Shippensburg University–Brenda Doyle, Joyce Yohe
Handley Library, Winchester, Virginia–Becky Ebert, Ben Ritter
Kittochtinny Library–Lillian Colletta, Hilary and Mona Mattingly
Pennsylvania Historical and Museum Commission–John Shelly and Lillian Ulrich
Pennsylvania State Law Library–Randall Tenor
Pennsylvania State Library–Lou Rauco
Shepherd College Library–Jean Elliott
Smithsonian Institution–Larry W. Vosloh
Washington County (MD) Free Library–John Frye, Ruth Kight, Kathleen O'Connell, Ann Reed
West Virginia Department of Culture and History - Carol Vandevender.

Individuals–Harvey C. Bridgers, Jr., Joan and Arthur Cordell, David Cline, Arben Harbaugh, Robert R. Peiffer, Leroy S. Maxwell, Sr., all the McClellans, wherever they may be, thanks to my wife, Pauline McClellan, Richard McClellan, Robert McClellan, and a special thanks to Elaine and Brian McClellan. *Betty Ramey, C. Omar Tracey, and C. Anderson Warner,* may God rest their souls.

Colonial Counterfeiters of the Blue Ridge

In May, 1697, William Penn wrote to the Provincial Council from London that, "There is no place more over-run with wickedness (than the Colony of Pennsylvania). Sins so very Scandalous, openly committed, in defiance of Law and Virtue; facts so foul than I am forbid by common modesty to relate ym."[1]

Pennsylvania was called in 1698, "Ye greatest refuge and shelter for pirates and rogues in America."[2] A colony founded on the principles of religion and the freedom of worship, our founding fathers were surprisingly lenient and ambivalent toward adopting suitable laws and codes involving criminal acts, although the Mother Country had held to extreme capital punishment for many years before. The governing council had since its inception been dominated by Quakers, the Society of Friends. This domination was influential in the Provincial government and took the lead to our modern ethic of opposition to war, slavery, and cruel corporal or capital punishment which involved death or flogging. Capital takes its name from *decapitation,* a form of execution. The Quakers were also the earliest to oppose feudal bondage and the irrational subjugation of the rights of women.

---

1 *Colonial Records of Pennsylvania,* Vol. I, p. 527, Letter of Feb. 9, 1697/8.
2 Loc Cit, p. 341.

As early as 1693, The Courts of the Counties were empowered to direct constables. In 1718, the Provincial Council went all out in setting up a capital code, that is, spelling out crimes punishable by death. This act of 1718 was designated **"An act for the advancement of justice and more certain administration thereof."** It spelled out thirteen capital crimes: treason, murder, manslaughter by stabbing, serious maiming, highway robbery, burglary, arson, sodomy, buggery, rape, concealing the death of a child, advising the killing of a child, and witchcraft. The Courts were directed to be made up of two Justices of the Supreme Court of the Commonwealth, assigned by the Honorable President and Supreme Executive Council, along with a select jury of twelve freemen to hear upon oath and affirmation of good and lawful men of the County in which such capital cases were tried. The President was given pardoning power but often left this to his Council, aided in their decision by the recommendation of the court of conviction; he also retained the power to stay an execution until adjudicated by royal instruction.[3]

You will notice that there is no mention of our subject, *counterfeiting,* in the above Act. By definition, counterfeiting is: to make anything in fraudulent imitation or similarity to something else and to represent it as genuine; to make or devise something spurious; to forge or falsify something.

The counterfeiting of money "must be the second oldest profession, for as soon as human beings became sufficiently

---

3   *Statutes-at-Large, Pennsylvania,* Vol. I, pp. 199-214.

social to have any sort of commercial interaction whatsoever, there was some shyster...trying to pass off as genuine an article of inferior worth."[4]

The coinage and printing of money were slow to develop in our colony, as was counterfeiting. Bartering one type of goods for another was the prevalent method of trade for a long time after settlement. As the colonies became more populous, if one did not have a commodity to offer in answer to his neighbor's need, he was hard put to trade for the things which he needed. This eventually led to the common acceptance of certain commodities—precious metals such as gold and silver of fixed, computed values—being tendered in exchange for a needed item. Foreign coinage served this purpose for a while, but the demand far exceeded the amount in circulation. In the estate of one of my ancestors, who died in Peters Township, Franklin County, PA. in 1747/8, there was inventoried, cash-in-hand: one Spanish Doubloon, five Spanish pieces of eight, one German caroline and twenty shillings of Maryland money.

In 1748, Pennsylvania Colony passed its first law governing the printing, signing and numbering of bills of credit; how they were to be signed, exchange of worn bills for new and how the old bills were to be disposed of. This law made it illegal to forge, counterfeit, or raise the denomination of any such bills so issued, under the punishment as set forth in former Acts.[5]

The former Acts dealt only with *forgery*. The penalty was to stand in and on a public pillory for the space of one hour in

---

4 Glaser, Lynn, *Counterfeiting in America*, Clarkson N. Potter, Crown, N.Y., 1968.
5 Loc Cit, Vol. V, p. 61.

midday, to suffer twenty-one lashes well laid on the bare back, to make restitution to the damaged party, pay a cash fine and stand the costs of prosecution.

Counterfeiting of these bills of credit and the altering of them became such a plague to the Colony that the punishment was made more stringent by the Acts of March 23, 1757 and May 29, 1767. The first provided that the altering of such bills be punishable by being pilloried, having both ears cut off and nailed to the pillory; to be publicly whipped thirty-one lashes; to forfeit a fine in amount of one hundred pounds lawful money of Pennsylvania, half to the use of the Governor, half to the discoverer; to make restitution in double the amount of damage done, and pay the costs of prosecution. If the offender could not pay, he could, by order of the Court, be sold for any term of indenture not exceeding seven years. The reward for discovery of an insolvent offender was reduced to five pounds, to be paid by the Province. The counterfeit bills were to be used in evidence and then burnt and destroyed by the Treasurer in the presence of a committee of the Supreme Council.[6]

By the time of passage of these Acts all the Colonies had paper currency and were issuing them with increasing frequency until after the Revolutionary War. The altering of denominations, sometimes known as "raising," was an increasing nuisance, and in some cases, so was the execution of the punishment.

---

6   Loc Cit, Vol. V, p. 300 and Vol. VII, p. 90.

A certain Miss Ann Tew, a spinster, was found guilty by a Lancaster County Court of altering a two-shilling note to ten shillings and then passing it off to Abraham Rinehart. Ann stood in the pillory for one hour, had both ears cut off and nailed to each side of the pillory, was given her thirty-one lashes and was required to pay a one-hundred-pound fine plus costs. Such a severe punishment, you would think, would be enough for anybody! Almost exactly one year later she was charged and found guilty of altering a one-shilling to a ten, and putting if off on a Mr. Gilbert. She received the same sentence as previous, which makes one wonder exactly how the executioner solved the problem of cutting off the ears already removed a year earlier.[7]

Finally, finally, in an Act of the general assembly passed on February 18, 1769, it was said that any person or persons shall presume to counterfeit any of the said Bills of Credit by printing in the likeness and similitude of the genuine, or forging the names of the signers of the true bills of credit, whether done in this province or elsewhere; or who shall utter such bills, knowing them to be counterfeit. (Uttering means passing or spending forged bills as true currency.) Such persons being legally convicted by confession, standing mute, or by verdict by twelve men in any court of oyer and terminer[8] within this province, he, she or they shall suffer death without

---

7 Scott Kenneth, *Counterfeiting in Colonial America,* Oxford University Press, N.Y., 1951, pp. 53-54.
8 *Oyer and Terminer* - (to hear and determine) A court of higher criminal jurisdiction. Reader's Digest Great Encyclopedic Dictionary, Pleasantville, N.Y., 1966, p. 966.

the benefit of clergy. The discoverer or informer of such a person shall have as encouragement, fifty pounds of the goods, chattels, lands and tenements of the convicted, and if no such value can be found, they shall have ten pounds, paid by the Province. Altering or raising bills was still punishable by the former act.

The *benefit of clergy* being simply the claim of exemption privilege from trial by civil court which was allowed to clergymen arraigned for felony, claiming the right to be tried by their peers in the Church in medieval England; in later times the privilege of exemption from the sentence, in the case of certain offenses, might be pleaded, on first offense by everyone who could read; the ability to read being merely a test of "clerkly," or clergy skills. The printed form of the fifty-first Psalm was set before the accused in black letter Latin, and if he could read it his neck would be saved. This was called in common parlance the "neck-verse."[9]

So much for the crime and the punishment thereof. What brought me to my curious involvement with the documentation of the Counterfeiters of the South Mountain was the accounts of, or, should I say, *veiled references* to, these men and their practices by county historians: Jacob H. Stoner and Benjamin Matthias Nead, both members of the Kittochtinny Historical Society, J. Thomas Scharf, landmark historian of Western Maryland, and Rev. Dr. Henry Harbaugh, eminent theologian, hymnist and native of Washington Township, Franklin County,

---

9   Oxford English Dictionary, Edit. Murray and others, Oxford Clarendon Press, 1933, pp. 66 and 104. See also Wharton's Law Lexicon, Stevens & Sons, Toronto, 1911.

PA. Among these four authors there is general agreement on one point: the era or time that the South Mountain events took place was between 1775 and 1804. There is agreement on some other points, but there is also confusion about the counties in which it all took place, those who took part (some writers do not even allude to their names, others give names totally in error), and some attempt to romanticize the counterfeiters' exploits.

Jacob Stoner stated in 1926 that "a short distance south of the Monterey Road (Washington Township, Franklin County) there is a cave or den frequented by a notorious gang engaged in imitating Continental Currency."[10] He relates how government officers, afraid to attack them in their den, went to the house of one and set it afire in an effort to induce him to forsake his hiding place, but to no avail. Later he was captured and lodged in the York County jail either on the pretext that the York Jail was a stronger prison or because the Congress was then in session there, about 1776 or 1777. Stoner neither names the criminal nor the officers of the law.

B. M. Nead, in his book *Waynesboro, a Centennial History,* states that "Well known through all this section of the county (Waynesboro?) was a notorious band of counterfeiters, highwaymen, and horse thieves, who operated from Virginia through the Cumberland, Lancaster and Chester Valleys. They were the Nugents, the Doanes and the Fritzes. So extensive was their network so as to furnish constant employment for agents all along the route even into Canada." He further relates how

---

10 Stoner, J. H., *Historical Papers,* Craft Press, Chambersburg, PA, 1947, p. 62.

vigilantes operated, "for it was the province of the brave settler to defend himself from every character of attack," under Colonel James Johnston and 'Squire' John Bourns to roust the desperadoes from the South Mountain.[11]

These men, in possession of a warrant from Carlisle, the county seat of Cumberland County, for the arrest of a counterfeiter and utterer, were scouring the South Mountain in search of him. Nead further relates how they had surrounded the swindlers' den in the dead of night, and after an all night vigil, there appeared on foot a man mistaken to be one of their own party in a military hat, who, failing to give the countersign, was pursued and captured by "Squire" Burns at bayonet point after a chase in which the pursued fell down and was quickly surrounded by Sheriff Johnston and the posse and marched down the mountain. James Johnston was High Sheriff of Cumberland County from 1779 to 1784. John Bourns or Burns was Magistrate of Antrim, Cumberland County, later Washington Township, Franklin County, beginning about the same time, 1779 until 1803.

J. Thomas Scharf in his *History of Western Maryland*, published in 1882, wrote quite a different story: "Valentine Shockey, son of Christopher Shockey, the patentee of 1800 acres, a small part of which was in this (then Frederick, now Washington County) and the balance in Pennsylvania, became a notorious counterfeiter. He flourished from about 1775 to 1804...he was a daring and desperate man...the boldest of the

---

11 Nead, Benj. M., *Waynesboro, A Centennial History*, Harrisburg, 1900, pp. 113-114.

counterfeiters who followed (on) the heels of the Revolution and his gang's exploits were known from Baltimore to the Ohio River..."[12]

Let us go to the source. In his *Annals of the Harbaugh Family*, Reverend Dr. Henry Harbaugh wrote that his father, George Harbaugh (1774-1853), bought 200 acres at the foot of Mount Misery (now called Mt. Quirauk at Pen Mar in the South Mountain range) from George's father Jacob Harbaugh, Sr., who had in turn purchased it earlier from Valentine Shockey on February 13, 1787. These two hundred acres were part of a Maryland grant made to Johann Christophel Shockey, father of Valentine, by Frederick, absolute lord and proprietary of the Province of Mary's Land.

The Reverend Henry Harbaugh states:

> "Shockey (Valentine) was a notorious counterfeiter. There is still a cave or den to be seen near Mt. Misery, east of the Great Falls on Falls Creek, which is called, "Shockey's Cave," where he and his confederates made their money and hid themselves in times when they were fearful of pursuit. This iniquitous business had been carried out along these mountains during the whole last quarter of the past century. Before my father bought that tract of land, Mr. Shockey resided on it. His house stood between the present house and the barn. On a certain occasion when a possee (sic) were in hot pursuit of the counterfeiter, they came to his house in the evening, but he had escaped to the mountain. They waited for some time and then set fire to his house, with the hope that the lurid sight would allure him from his hidding (sic) and if he should come to rescue his house they might be able to capture him. The flames soon raged and struck forth

---

[12] Scharf, J. Thomas A.M., *History of Western Maryland*, 1882, Vol. I, p. 614.

fearfully from the doomed house—the family having, of course, been allowed to escape. On the woods around and upon the mountains more distant, shone the red glare of the burning house. The possee (sic) lay in ambush, watchful and silent, but the old fox was too wise to be called forth by such a ruse. From the side of the mountain he saw with stoic calmness how the fire was turning his home into flames and smoke and ashes. Better no house and freedom, than to fall into prison in a vain attempt to save it. The exploits of this terrible gang of which Shockey was the leader, would make quite a chapter of wicked daring if collected and recorded. Shockey's Cave and its traditions will not soon pass from the memory of the generations in that region of the country...we remember as a boy, to have turned up with a harrow in the plowed meadow, a zinc plate, the counterfeit type of a Continental note. Shockey was in the York County Jail at the time grandfather bought the land from him (in the year 1787, as before stated)."[13]

Mt. Misery, Falls Creek, South Mountain, counterfeiters, cave or den, Continental Currency, Congress in session in York. It all seems plausible—with several exceptions and some reservation— here are four local historians writing more or less independently of each other, in 1846, in 1882, in 1897 and in 1926, yet at variance with each other over details that could have been verified. Had they ignored each other; had they researched the actual facts?

Then there was the matter of the cave or den. Inquire as I might, I could not locate it. Over the years I asked many local people, professional and laymen alike, who knew these parts of South Mountain and knew them well. Yes, they knew of the

---

13 Harbaugh, Henry Rev., *Annals of the Harbaugh Family*, 1st Edition, privately printed, 1856, p. 69ff.

counterfeiters, even called them by name. Would it be possible to show me the cave or den? By all means, the next time we get up that way driving or hunting or hiking, or after mushroom hunting, we will show it to you. Almost all of those asked stayed true to their word, except when they went seeking, all of them to a man failed to find it! Some pointed out places at wide geographical variance with each other; others went to the general vicinity but could not find it exactly. Their father or brother or uncle had shown them years ago and "it's right around here, if they were here they could show you where it is."

This was too much! Either the place existed or it didn't! Its location, so remote and so mysterious, aroused my curiosity with each vain attempt and each passing year.

Someday I would pursue the story of these Shockey counterfeiters and locate their hidden den.

James Johnston and Squire John Burns had, in the early morning light, taken into custody and transported to the Cumberland Jail, in Carlisle, a young soldier named Christopher Shockey, the youngest brother of the leader of the band and some seventeen years Valentine's junior. Chris most probably did wear a military hat, because he was fresh from three years' service in the Command of Col. Thomas Hartley, the Seventh Pennsylvania Regiment of the Continental Line. This battalion, from the camp at Trappe, had seen action at Paoli, Brandywine, and Germantown. They had lost 300 privates to British bayonets and returned with four Captains, three Lieutenants and only 87 private soldiers. This battalion was reorganized into the new Eleventh Regiment. Colonel Hartley resigned on 13 February 1779, and the veterans, of whom young Christopher Shockey was one, were discharged of their duty.[14]

There is no way for us to know whether or not young Shockey's wife was involved in passing counterfeit money as he was, but women and children were of great use to counterfeiters, for they were less often suspected of spending bogus money. Surprisingly few women were punished, even upon conviction, for uttering bad money—altering, yes, but not uttering. Both women and children were usually involved for trifling gain and, as adept as they were, women were given a choice of paying a fine and costs or standing corporal punishment. Their family generally came to the rescue by raising the fine, costs and restitution. Of the two dozen odd women that were executed by hanging in Pennsylvania, well over three-fourths of them were executed not for counterfeiting or uttering, but rather for murder or infanticide.

Christopher Shockey's story began when he returned home from the Continental service in February of 1779. He was a young but hardened soldier. He had seen much hard living and hard fighting at the hands of the British. He was lucky to be alive. Now, he was going to live a little. From his brothers he must have either borrowed or bought, at less than face value, some Continental bills of credit, and headed straightaway into Carlisle, the county town. At the shop of Michael Miller, a

---

14 *Colonial Record,* Fifth Series, Vol. VI.

hosier and clothier on the east side of Hanover Street two doors north of Lowther Street, he probably bought himself a complete suit of clothes, new from head to toe. From thence to the barber shop of Joseph Sabole (Sabbole) for a bath, a shave, and a haircut. Sabole's shop was on the south side of Lowther Street, midway between Bedford and East Streets.

This shop and house of Sabole had been, in December of 1777, the scene of a patriotic encounter between Edmond Kean and John Gibson and one Richard Stack, Drum and Fife Major of the Seventh Battalion of the Pennsylvania Line. Edmond Kean said, according to the deposition of Joseph Sabole and others, "God damn all those who would leave fighting for the King to wear the coat you now have on," and had said, "God damn you and all that join you!" John Gibson had said, "God damn General Washington," which he repeated two or three times. This altercation and the above depositions were intended to show treason on the part of Kean and Gibson, but investigation has shown nothing in the way of charges being brought.[15]

After visiting the barber and the clothier, Christopher was all dressed up and ready for a night on the town. The only place that we have record of him going was near Carlisle Square, a few doors east of the Episcopal Church and Irvine's Row—the tavern kept by William Holmes in the High Street. We might assume the visit went something like this: "Drinks all around, Christly's back from the War and damned lucky to be here by the bargain." We do not know whether he got drunk

---

15 Clerk of Courts Records, Manuscript [32-17] 1777, Hamilton Library, Cumberland County Historical Society, Carlisle, PA.

or not; he was not lodged in the jail a short distance away. Perhaps he was just hungry!

The one thing we are sure of is that there was a great hue and cry the following morning, April 24, 1779, at the offices of High Sheriff James Johnston of Cumberland County, when Messrs. Miller, Sabole, and William Holmes (the tavern keeper) arrived to announce that they were collectively holding 34 pieces of counterfeit paper $30 bills of the emission dated 22 July 1776, passed on to them all by the same man—Christopher Shockey. Couldn't you venture a guess—he was not to be found in the town of Carlisle! A warrant was sworn out, both for counterfeiting and uttering counterfeit money, to take young Shockey into custody. As described earlier, he was finally captured at the hideout in South Mountain in September, 1779, and was imprisoned in Carlisle.[16]

He was an inmate in the Stone Jail, which was erected in 1754-55 at the northeast corner of High and Bedford Streets. This Jail was reported on to the "Worshipfull Justices of the Quarter Sessions by the Grand Jury of the County of Cumberland, John Holmes, Foreman" in the July Sessions preceding Shockey's arrest (1778) as having been viewed as requested and the Grand Jurors did present that: "The Gaol, (sic) both upstairs and below insufficient for securing the prisoners that are or may be put therein, in the first place it wants a new roff (sic) and that roff (sic) lined with two-inch plank, secondly, the garret floor wants considerable repair, also

---

16 Pennsylvania Historical and Museum Commission, Division of Archives and Manuscripts, Harrisburg, RG-27, Roll 36.

a good well is much wanted, these with any necessary repairs that the Commissioners for said county may think proper may render the prison for said county sufficient for some time.[17]

By the time Shockey arrived there, the jail must have been sufficiently repaired, because the Grand Jury for the Quarter Sessions of July, 1779, the following year, reported "(we) do present that there (sic) being requested by the High Sheriff of said County to examine and view said Goal (sic) and finds it sufficient for the security of prisoners there confined and the Inquest desires that this be put on record." Again it was signed, John Holmes, Foreman.[18] I suppose there was some security for both the Court and Commissioners in having the same Grand Jurors sit in Sessions in perpetuity.

It appears the jail had been made so secure that Chris had lost his chance to escape. Oh, well! They probably would have captured him again anyway!

Now that the criminal is safely incarcerated, let us discuss some astounding events of significance not only to him, but also to the citizens-at-large in all the thirteen colonies united into one nation.

After the beginning of the Revolution, the Continental Congress found itself powerless to supply, much less pay, an army and stand the expense of running the government. The individual states collected their own taxes and had their own governments to run, and found that their revenue would not

---

17 Grand Jury Reports 1778, Manuscript, Hamilton Library, Cumberland County Historical Society, Carlisle, PA.
18 Ibid., 1779.

bear contributing to the administration of a central government. The obvious answer was to issue bills of credit, such as the King they were rebelling against had demanded of them, i.e., Continental Currency with no backing except the name of the United States and the promise to pay in gold or silver. The policy and opinion of the public in our country, as has been shown, was still strongly divided between the British and the rebellious American colonists.

The British were quick to grasp the opportunity and flooded the colonies with counterfeit currency, knowing full well the feeble credit upon which Continental dollars were based. They imported shipboard printing presses and false "Congress Notes" through the ports their ships were blockading. They produced some excellent emissions; some looked more genuine than the genuine, the British bills being made from engraved plates, while the Continentals were made up in set type. They approached paper manufacturers (one of them was in Chambersburg) to try to obtain a quantity of approved ising-glass or mica paper, but were rebuffed. They found the needed paper by stealing it and capturing a number of wagonloads in shipment. Continental currency continued to depreciate at an alarming rate. It became so worthless that had it not been for the financial gymnastics of Robert Morris and Benjamin Franklin, we probably would not have found the wherewithal to become an independent nation at all!

General George Washington, he who had sacrificed everything for the cause, was constantly exhorting Congress to put a stop to counterfeiting within and without our borders. He wrote to the President of the Continental Congress from his Morristown headquarters:

> "I have inclosed a copy of an Advertisement published in Gaines Paper of the 14th, which shows that no artifices are left untried by the enemy to injure us. Before the appearance of this unparalleled piece, I had heard that a person was gone from York to Rhode Island with a quantity of Counterfeit Money."[19]

I offer this letter from the Archives of Maryland:

> Delegates in Congress to Governor Johnson
> Philadelphia. Sep. 26, 1779
> Sir, Your Excellency will be informed by the enclosed deposition of a number of villains in the State of Maryland and Virginia concerned in Counterfeiting the currency of the United States. As secrecy and expedition are necessary to bring these wretches to punishment, we have not the least doubt but that your Excellency and the Country will adopt such measures you may deem necessary for accomplishing this end and are with the greatest respect and esteem,
> Sir,
> Your Excellency's most obt. servants,
> (S)William Paca
> (S)William Carmichael
> (S)James Forbes
> (S)Daniel of St. Thomas Jenifer
>
> P.S. The enclosed letters referred to the MD. Delegation who have not been able to get information of any such man in our State. They therefore refer the same to your Excellency and Council. The Count De Staigne (sic) with his fleet are off Georgia.[20]

---

19 Fitzpatrick, John C., Ed., *The Writings of George Washington*, Washington, D.C., 1931, Vol. VII, p. 434.

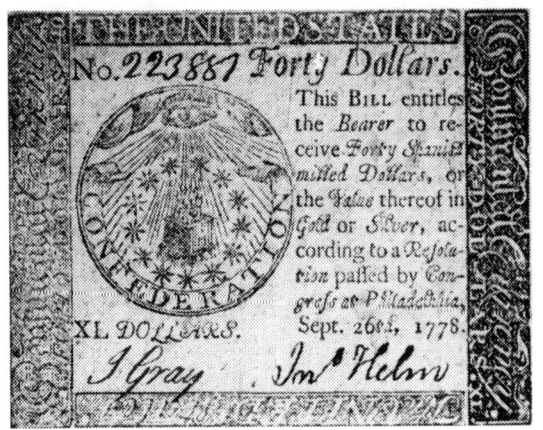

Genuine US Paper $40 Bill

Counterfeit $40 Bill

Smithsonian Institution-National Numismatic Collection PHOTO

Note the difference in sharpness and clarity of impression of the two. The bogus bill, probably British, is obviously the better strike.

Count d'Estaing (1729-1794) was a French admiral mercenary, ill-treated while a British prisoner in 1759. He obtained command of an American fleet and set about to drive the British fleet from America. He blockaded Lord Howe in New York Harbor and then set sail for the West Indies where he captured strategic islands. At the time of this information his fleet was enroute to Savannah to attack the British blockade, but he was repulsed, suffered heavy losses and returned to France in 1780. If not in complete disgrace, he was certainly mortified![21]

The deposition so discreetly conveyed was an instrument of examination of a Cumberland County man, which was executed in Yorktowne, York County, Pennsylvania, before Justices of the Peace David Jamieson and William Scott.

It was the deposition of Mark Milligan of Black's Gap, near Pond Bank and Caledonia, who stood accused of a misdemeanor of having Counterfeiting Stamps in his possession. It was a lesser charge to make and have the plates, than to print with them. Milligan pleaded guilty to the charge, but in making this plea he bargained for leniency by agreeing to "roll-over" or give information on those he knew were engaged in the money business and he wasn't going to tell all about bankers!

What Mark Milligan said was most revealing:

> "The examination of Mark Milligan, late of Cumberland Township in the County of York, taken the 10th day of September in the year 1779, Who says that about three years

---

20 Published Archives of Maryland, Vol. XXI, pp. 537-538, and in part Cong. IV, p. 441.
21 Encyclopaedia Brittanica, 1961 Edition Vol. 8, pp. 727-728, Vol. 22, p. 787.

ago (1776) Isaac and Abraham Shockey and John Dutterow came to the examinant at this home in Black's Gap and said they knew he could engrave and requested him to engrave plates for them to counterfeit money; that he engraved plates of eight dollar bills and that John Dutterow paid this examinant £30 for them. That said Dutterow lives sometimes at Shockey's and sometimes at his brother's about 20 miles from Shockey's in the State of Maryland.

That two years ago, (1777) this examinant was applied to by Joseph Nicholson of Nicholson's Gap, York County (now Adams County, near Blue Ridge Summit) and John King, since a soldier, to engrave plates for them to counterfeit money. That he engraved a plate to strike five dollar bills and a plate to strike seven dollar bills, for which they paid near £150...Sometime after, Valentine Shockey applied to him for two thirty dollar stamps for which he received £50 apiece. (The Chief Justice has one of his (Milligan's) notes from a plate for a large $8). That afterwards he was taken up and admitted to bail by the Chief Justice; that he was applied to about the latter part of April (1779) by Abraham and Isaac Shockey to make prints of the forty dollar plates, now in the possession of Mr. Archibald McClean, but that he put them off, under some pretence (sic) and did not do it for them. That a family by the name of Cook, who lived in Black Water, in the State of Virginia have a press and strike counterfeit money...That Valentine Shockey and Isaac Shockey applied to this examinant to go a sign money for the Cooks. That "Felty" (Valentine) Shockey signs their own emissions and he saw the Shockeys strike their money different times. That they do it with an instrument like a lemonsqueezer.

That James Thompson of Conococheague, near to James Campbell's Tavern has a bill of Felty Shockey's making and signing. That Hugh Welsh, who served part of his time with Clerk (Clark) near Black's Gap has a quantity of Shockey's money...That all the Newgents (sic) are concerned with the

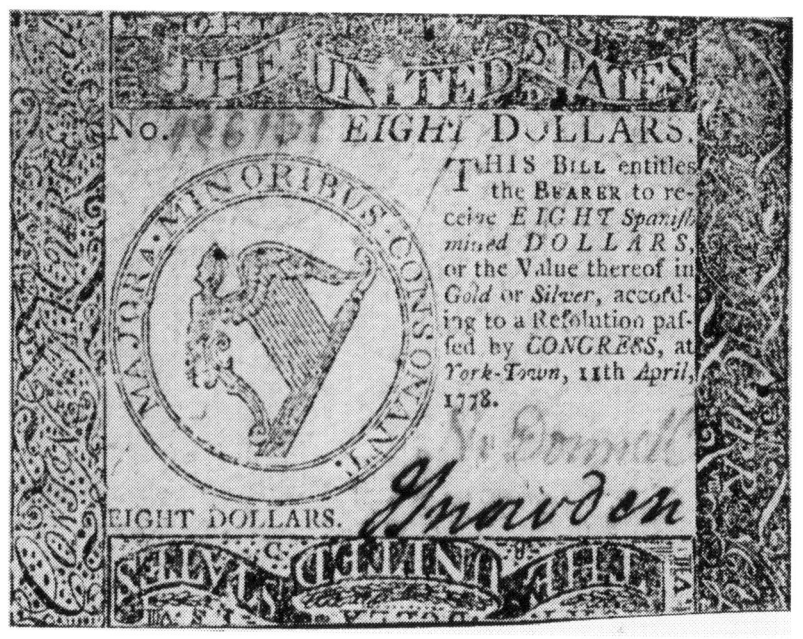

Smithsonian Institution-National Numismatic Collection PHOTO

Genuine Large $8 US

Photo of a Large $8 bill referred to in engraver Mark Milligan's deposition implicating the Shockey's in counterfeiting.

Shockeys and pass their money. That one Roseburgh (sic) who lives in the Mountain is concerned with the Shockeys and passes their money..."22

(S) Mark Milliken

Taken and Subscribed the day and year aforesaid before
David Jameson
Wm. Scott

Milligan had said enough, perhaps too much for the comfort of his shady clientele, but he got himself off, being sentenced for having plates in his possession to stand in the pillory in Yorktowne for one hour on the 8th day of November, 1779, between the hours of ten and twelve in the forenoon and to be confined to the York County Gaol until the next Fourth of July, the anniversary of Independence; pay a fine of £2000; give security himself in the amount of £3000 and provide one good security, other than himself, in the amount of £1500, for his good behavior and that he keep the peace to all the Liege subjects of the Commonwealth during the present war, and pay the costs of prosecution. The flogging was expediently omitted.

Milligan lived to stand before the Court on a later day. His deposition put some of the questions about our South Mountain men into perspective and started an all out search for and an ostensible government purge of counterfeiters. That didn't move any faster then than it does now, and carried forward from the day of testimony for at least twenty-five years thereafter.

Milligan made no mention of Christopher Shockey and it is doubtful that he was a member of Valentine, Isaac and Abraham's

---

22 Maryland State Papers (Red Books)#5, MD AR4563, Item 43. Manuscript.

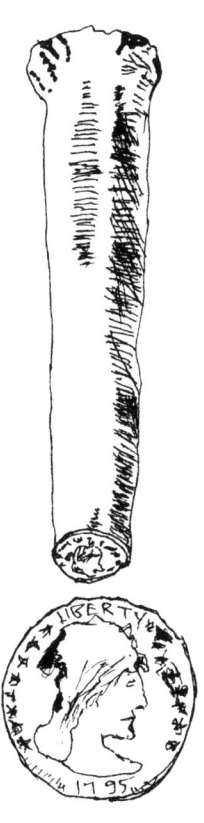

Crude Die Stamp

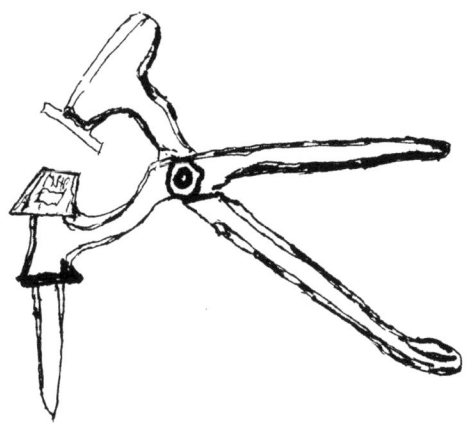

Portable "Lemon Squeezer" Press

ring. It is my opinion that Christopher Shockey was an utterer and got caught within the circle of fire touched off by the testimony of Mark Milligan.

The young ex-soldier, Shockey, was denied bond as surety for his appearance before the October Session Court of Oyer and Terminer in Cumberland County held at Carlisle. Many others taken into custody on the strength of Milligan's deposition (bad news has a way of traveling fast) were charged with counterfeiting and uttering, and were released on their own recognizance to appear at the October Court.

Joseph Nicholson, mentioned by Milligan, charged with passing counterfeit money knowingly, and being called for arraignment, failed to appear, thereby forfeiting his bond and that of James Brotherton's and John Sullivan. James Nugent, also fingered by Milligan, charged with passing counterfeit knowingly, and being three times solemnly called, failed to appear, and thereby forfeited the bonds in all of five men. Benjamin Nugent, charged with arson, being three times called and not appearing, forfeited his own bond and that of Moses Lamb, John Vance, and John Sullivan. Sullivan lost twice in one day! William Lumley and John Rosborough were free on £10,000 bond to answer the charge of Felony in Counterfeiting and Uttering Knowingly, and were to appear at the next session of the Court.[23]

A Grand Jury found a true bill against Christopher Shockey on the 18th day of October, 1779, on the charge of Counterfeiting and Uttering Knowingly thirty-four (34) pieces

---

23 Pennsylvania Historical and Museum Commission, Division of Archives and Manuscripts, Harrisburg, PA RG-27-Roll 36.

of paper in the similitude of the emission of $30 bills issued by the Honorable Continental Congress on the 22nd of July, 1776, the crime being perpetrated on 23 April 1779.[24]

The trial came on the 20th day of October, before the Supreme Court of the Commonwealth, Thomas McKean, Chief Justice and William Augustus Attlee, 2nd Justice, Presiding.

A jury of twelve good, free and lawful men of the County was drawn. The prisoner was in the custody of Sheriff James Johnston, his captor. Edward Burd, Clerk of the Courts for Cumberland County, was Prosecutor for the Commonwealth and defense attorney. Shockey, having put himself for good or evil upon God, the Country, and the Jury, entered a plea of *not guilty*. The Jury, having heard the testimony of the damaged parties, returned a verdict of not guilty of counterfeiting, but guilty of uttering counterfeit money knowingly. The prisoner, being questioned if he had or knew anything further to say in his own behalf or any reason why Judgment should not be passed against him, said nothing further. It was considered the judgment of the Court that the said Christopher Shockey be hanged by the neck till he be dead.[25]

A warrant for the execution of Christopher Shockey was issued under the lesser Seal of the Commonwealth on November 23, 1779, after His Excellency Joseph Reed, President, and the Supreme Executive Council heard the petitions of sundry inhabitants in or near the Town of Carlisle for lenience on behalf of the condemned. These were read and duly considered. The

---

24   Ibid, RG-27, Roll 36 p. 47, 56.
25   Ibid, RG-27, Roll 36, Frame 906.

date of execution of the sentence of death was set for Saturday, the eleventh day of December, in the same year. It was also warranted that the sentence of death by hanging be carried out upon Thomas Madden for Highway Robbery, and Thomas Story for Murder at the same place and time.

There were a number of petitions for Mercy in Shockey's behalf, all given under one heading:

Petition

We, the subscribers, in consideration of the helpless state of the within named prisoner's family as well as of his former service as a soldier in the Continental Service, do beg leave to recommend him to your Excellency, the President and Supreme Executive Council as an object of mercy, in Carlisle, 26 October 1779.

I do know the within named Christopher Shockey to have been a good and faithfull (sic) soldier in Colonel Hartley's Regiment.

(S) Chas. Lukens

Charles Lukens (1746-1784) was the Sheriff of York County from 1774 to 1778, and took command of Colonel Hartley's Regiment upon his resignation in 1779. He was a Major, acting Colonel, at Carlisle Barracks at this time, and Shockey had never served directly under him.

I do sartyfy (sic) that Christopher Shockey behaved himself well when in my custody.

(S) Matthew Atkinson, Gaoler (sic)

We, the undersigned subscribers, do sartify (sic) yt we have lived neighbors to sd Christopher Shockey and had business with him and never knew him to pass or offer to pay any counterfeit money before he was apprehended in Carlisle.

>   (S) Wm. Morrison
>   John Warden
>   Peter Psalbo (Sabole)
>   Andw. McManes
>   Hendrick Darby
>   Christopher Plummer [26]

The petitioner neighbors of Christopher Shockey lived in that part of Cumberland County, soon to become Franklin County, in Chamberstown, then Franklin Township, or in the adjoining Hamilton Township.

The Petition of Christopher Shockey now in the Jail in Carlisle

Most Humbly Sheweth (sic): That your petitioner has been indicted and convicted for having passed counterfeit money and has received Judgment of Death.

Your petitioner has been three years a soldier in Col. Hartley's Regiment in the Continental Service and during that period has fully discharged his duty as a soldier and would continue to render his services in that way to his Country. But, his present deplorable situation prevents him and having a wife and three small children, he most earnestly solicits and prays for your Honour's clemency and mercy and that your Honours, in consideration of his past service and helpless family will grant him a pardon of his offense and of the awful penalty to which he is sentenced.

And your petitioner will is as Duty bound pray,

>   (S) Christopher Shockey
>   Unhappy Brother in the Temple of Fame[27]

Carlisle Jail
26 October, 1779

---

26 Pennsylvania Historical and Museum Commission, Division of Archives and Manuscripts, Harrisburg, PA, Clemency File, 1779.

27 Ibid.

"The Temple of Fame" being an allusion to the Court's sentence of death when passed upon a prisoner "of *evil name and Fame*. Christopher Shockey was saying that had his last name not been Shockey he would not be under the death penalty. Fame has its rewards and its penalties. "The Temple of Fame is the shortest passage to riches and preferment,"[28] and then, too, "The temple of Fame, stands upon the grave: the flame that burns upon its altar is kindled from the ashes of dead men."[29]

These pleas and cries begging for mercy on Shockey's behalf carried little weight or influence. His brothers' past had made him a man of "evil name and fame."[30] He was a Shockey. That name and reputation was voiced throughout the countryside. His kinfolk were not able to help him for fear that they too would be taken into custody. Showing themselves would jeopardize all. We would be the last to claim that Christopher was an innocent victim of circumstance. He was a member of the family and had dealt with them long enough to be aware of what they were about and the risks involved in their type of business. We must admit that he had gone into hiding and had evaded his captors for four or five months. In my opinion, he was executed as an *example* to all others engaged in debasing the currency of our nation at a most critical time.

As appointed, Christopher Shockey took his "long step" on the 11th day of December, along with Story and Madden, upon

---

28 Anon, Letters of Junius, London, 1772.
29 Hozlelt, Wm., Lectures on the English Poets, Lecture #8.
30 Pennsylvania Historical and Museum Commission, RG-27-Roll 36.

the gallows by the jailyard in the Carlisle town square. These executions had become almost carnival in atmosphere; that's why they were scheduled on Market Day. Everybody came to town. The prisoners "were taken out midst a Crowd of Spectators—they walked after a cart in which were...their coffins...their arms were tied behind them...generally they were accompanied by their family, wife, sisters and mother, and a clergyman. Loui (Lewis) Miller, who went from York to Lancaster to see an execution describes it thus: The gallows had a tremendous trapdoor on the platform. And when the Sheriff give (sic) the word the trapdoor fell. Oh! What a crowd to see a poor sinner of a creature at the gallows."[31]

> "They were made occasions for large gatherings from far and near, mostly bent on idle curiosity, or for a grand jollification, and some even bent on attempts to rescue the prisoner. They came by wagons, on horseback and on foot, in constantly increasing proportions down to the moment of the execution. Many came long distances, arriving the night before, crowding the taverns the preceding evening, or sleeping in wagons...on the road to the place, booths were erected for the sale of confectionaries, eatables and intoxicants...The presence of the military was always required to prevent turbulence..."[32]

What had started for Chris Shockey as a lark, ended in doom! Those members of his brother Valentine's infamous gang of outlaws that were arrested at the same time as Christopher, but failed to appear for arraignment, ended up on the gallows.

---

31 Teeters, Negley K., *Public Executions in Pennsylvania*, 1682- 1834 Lancaster County Historical Society V. 64, No. 2, 1960.
32 Ibid, p. 25.

In Cumberland County, James and Benjamin Nugent, a reward of £1000 placed on each of their heads by Joseph Reed, President of the Supreme Executive Council, were tried in Carlisle on May 22, 1780, for Highway Robbery, and went to their deaths on the same hanging tree as Christopher Shockey on 17 June 1780.[33]

The Doanes, Abraham and Levi, cousins, not brothers (as they were commonly called) were executed in Philadelphia County, September 24, 1788. These men had been outlawed since 1781 and thus were executed without a trial.[34]

As for Valentine Shockey, his life of crime went on as before. Milligan and Rosborough were still around, as well as Christian Hoover. The crime of counterfeiting and uttering had now become, in the eyes of the Country and its people, a "disloyal act, akin to treason." It is interesting to follow the wavering stringency and leniency of the attitudes of the citizens and the Courts being held toward certain criminal matters, depending upon the circumstances of the times.

Such was the case of Christian Hoover, who stood convicted in York County, of the Felony of Uttering Counterfeit Money Knowingly on October 29, 1779—this about two weeks after Christopher Shockey was sentenced to death for committing the same crime. Hoover had about the same amount of testimony against him *plus* a confession made by himself, but he claimed the benefit of clergy, even though contrary to the Act, and it was granted to him. He was branded with the letter

---

33 *Colonial Record of Pennsylvania*, Vol. XII, p. 261, p. 375.
34 Ibid, Vol. IV, p. 505, 515, 535.

"T" in the brawn of his left thumb and sentenced to be committed to the County Gaol of York until the second Tuesday in October following, an incarceration of about one year, and to pay costs of prosecution.[35]

The tradition had been handed down that Valentine Shockey wore his hair long. It was possible that

> "long hair and wigs had their ulterior uses in colonial days when ear-cropping was thus rife. Romantic tales of life on the road tell of carefully hidden deformities, of mysteriously gauntleted strangers, whose hands, when displayed, revealed the lurid brand of past villainies. Life was cramped and dull in those days, but there were diversions; when breezes might lift the locks from your friend or lover's cheek and give a glimpse of a ghastly hole instead of an ear or display a burning letter on their forehead; their shoulder, under a lace collar might have been branded by a rogues mark or their back branded with scars and welts of fierce lashes of the cat-o-nine tails.[36]

We have found no evidence that Valentine ever had his ears cropped or had been branded, and we next find him on the public record in a Cumberland County deposition of Benjamin Musselman, who stood accused of feloniously stealing, taking, and carrying away (Larceny) of four yards and a half of callico (sic), value of £300; 6 yards and a half of striped linnen (sic), valued at £200 and five yards of Shantung of the value of £100, lawful money of Pennsylvania. The true bill against Musselman sworn as the goods and chattels of James McCuen was found

---

35 Pennsylvania Historical and Museum Commission, Division of Archives and Manuscripts. Harrisburg, PA RG-27-York Co. 1779.
36 Earle, Alice Morse, *Curious Punishments of Bygone Days*, Chicago, 1896.

the 10th day of September, 1780.[37] Musselman had decided to "chirp up" on the 27th day of August 1780:

> *"The examination of Benj. Musselman of Washington Township Cumberland County saith that early this spring at the house of Abram Derush (a tipling house) in said township, he met Felty Shockey, that he, the said Musselman, went out of the house and said Shockey followed him out and showed him a bundle of money; that this examinant said to Shockey, he had a good deal of money and said to him in a joking manner, "I wish you would give me some of it." and that Shockey asked him, said examinant, if he had any linnen (sic) cloth to sell, who answered he had not; that Shockey told him he would give him all the money for three yards and he would trust him till he could buy it, that accordingly, he the deponent, took the money from Shockey and that shortly afterwards Shockey came to his house and got three yards of linnen (sic), that he the said examinant paid a thirty dollar bill of the money he got of Shockey to John Ormsby, which bill was returned by Ormsby as a counterfeit bill, that he also payd (sic) one thirty and one forty dollar bill (of said money) to Mr. Jack, a blacksmith, which was also returned as bad money, that he likewise offered to Andrew Thompson in Peters Township some of said money in pay for some tow cloth, which was refused, that he payd (sic) a thirty or forty dollar bill to a man whose name he forgets for some whisky, which bill was not returned, that finding the money he got of Shockey would not pass, he come home (sic) and burned the bills that was returned by Mr. Jack and that going to the Mill, he found some of said money he got from Shockey in his pocket, which he threw in the woods that this examinant told Shockey when he offered him so much money for three yards cloth that he thought it was not good, that Shockey said that it was as good as any money, that Shockey afterwards offered to lend him more money, that he, Musselman, refused to take anymore,*

---

37 Hamilton Library Cumberland County Historical Society, Clerks of the Courts Record Manuscript. 32-17 (1780).

said he throw'd (sic) away what he got before of him.
       Taken and acknowledged, 27th Aug 1780
       Before Us
              John Agnew
              Samuel Laird
     (S) Benjamin Musselman [38]

There is no indication of record in Cumberland County that any action was taken on the basis of this information. Next we find Valentine Shockey cited for Keeping a Tipling House without a recommendation or license; that is: selling or delivering quantities of rum, whiskey, brandy, beer, cider and other strong and spiritous liquors by less measure than one quart. A warrant was issued for his arrest to appear before the Court of Quarter Sessions, January 1789, to answer the charge. The record indicates nothing further.

Valentine Shockey and his cohorts were well connected and believe me, they covered the ground! In 1787, Valentine and an accomplice, having changed over to the manufacture of hard currency (paper money having become worthless), were taken into custody in Franklin Township, York County, (now Adams County) Pennsylvania, that township between Caledonia Iron Furnace and Cashtown. They were taken into custody for using pewter, lead and other base metals to make coins in similar form and likeness to silver French crowns, quarters of Spanish milled dollars, Spanish milled dollars and Portuguese pistereens. These coins were all like the silver coins still being used in the Commonwealth.

---

[38] Ibid, Manuscript Records 32-17.

It was about this time, you will remember, that Rev. Henry Harbaugh stated that his grandfather bought the land in Washington Township, Franklin County, PA, near Harbaugh's Church, from Valentine, who was then in jail in York County.

From the record at this point in time, it appears that Felty Shockey spent as much time in jail as he did outside of it. He was indicted, along with Philip Nagle, on the last mentioned charge, which case was dropped in May 1787. The charge was changed to Suspicion of Making and Passing Counterfeit Money. The charge against Nagle remained the same as before. Valentine Shockey's charge was changed to passing counterfeit money on testimony of Wm. McMunn, Moses Ely, and John Eley. The trial came on the 11th of June, 1788. The jury returned a verdict of not guilty of passing; ordered that Valentine be discharged from the indictment, that he pay the costs and post £400 surety, and that he provide two freeholders as surety in the amount of £200 each for his appearance at Court next session.[39]

Guess who else was in York County Jail at the same time? John Rosborough was jailed for passing counterfeit money; and Mark Milligan and Wm. Robinson were both incarcerated for Felony in Receiving Stolen Goods, Accessories before and after the fact in Burglary, and Larceny respectively. Nagle was in on all of the above charges plus making counterfeit money.

On June 12, 1788, Valentine returned to Court and stood trial for felony counterfeiting and was acquitted.[40] His

---

39 Pennsylvania Historical and Museum Commission, Division of Archives and Manuscripts. Record Group 27; York Co. 1787-88.

accomplice, Philip Nagle, upon being tried for making Spanish milled dollars, etc., at the same place and time, was found guilty. His sentence: that he be hung by the neck until he be dead. Shockey walked away again!

Nagle was to be hanged on the 8th day of July, 1788, at the usual place of execution in York. His death warrant was considered in the Executive Council at the same time as that of "Negro" Jack Durham's execution in Franklin County for rape in Southampton Township.

In the Council, June 30, 1788, the case of Philip Nagle was reconsidered as to a stay of execution. The reconsideration was the result of the Council's attempts to investigate allegations that were made through two petitions received by Hon. Benjamin Franklin, Esq., President of the Supreme Executive Council from a number of (20 or 21) mostly Quaker ladies of York in favor of leniency toward Philip Nagle. These petitions stated, in general:

> "that the condemned prisoner was young and under hardship, and that his execution would cast a pall upon "the approaching anniversary day which gave us freedom and for the adoption of a government which promises to establish and secure peace, liberty and happiness to every Federal Son of America, and that a certain Valentine Shockey, who stood indicted for the same crime and against whom the facts were more plainly proven is found not guilty by a Jury of the County...and the prisoner conceives that the crime for which he stands convicted is not within the letter or meaning of the law, as it was not proven that he had any intention to pass the money.

---

40 Ibid.

The petition humbly prays that the severity of punishment be lessened and hopes he be considered an object of Mercy by your Honorable President and Body."[41]

The President and Council decided not to spoil the Anniversary of our Country's Independence; Nagle's hanging was postponed until July 19th, 1788. As for the others, Wm. Robinson got 14 years at hard labor; Mark Milligan drew 10 years on the wheelbarrow, and John Rosborough's charges were dropped.[42]

Valentine Shockey quit the county after this close encounter in York. He sold out and went south into Frederick County, Virginia. He no doubt was well acquainted with the Cooks, the infamous Virginia printers. He settled in the area of Bath (Berkeley Springs), which had long been an "infamous place" as a resort and good place for a confidence man to practice his tricks and trade. The other Shockeys had scattered; Valentine, first to Bath and then to the head of Sleepy Creek (now Morgan County, West Virginia); Abraham, his brother, went into the Ohio Territory; Isaac migrated further into Virginia, and then perhaps, Kentucky Territory.

There is no indication that Valentine gave up his business of moonshining, counterfeiting, uttering and went "straight," but he avoided the "long arm" of the law for quite a time after he left Pennsylvania. Although he was around, the record shows him involved in estate proceedings in 1796, 1797, 1800 and 1802.

---

41 Ibid, R. G. 27 Roll 40, also PA Col. Records V. XV, p. 483.
42 *Pennsylvania Colonial Records,* Vol. XV, p. 483.

It is possible he operated further west with his brothers. It is more likely he stuck to the hills of Virginia "where the sun don't shine" (now the hills of West Virginia).

Then it happened, as we knew it would all along!

Maryland Herald And Elizabethtown Weekly Advertiser
Vol. IV, No. 308, Page 3-D, Weds. January 19, 1803
Now Hagerstown, Washington County, Maryland

Martinsburg, January 14

Money-Makers

"*For some time past, suspicions were entertained, that base money was made in the shop of a certain William Streithoff, near Sleepy Creek, in this County. To realize these suspicions and detect the persons engaged in this nefarious procedure, a party of persons surrounded the shop on Friday last. The shop was found closed. One of the party approached near the door when he distinctly heard the jingle of money. They demanded admittance, the demand was not complied with, the door was then forced upon, when four men, apparently much dismayed were discovered. These men were Comsey, Dawson, Streithoff and the far-famed and well-known* **Shockey**. *Many base dollars were found, together with a number of crucibles, a quantity of necessary ingredients for preparing the metal and all the implements for coining dollars. The four persons were then arrested and brought to Martinsburg Jail.*

Their trial came on yesterday, before the Court of Enquiry, in this town, when the Court after examining the witnesses and hearing the pleadings against and in favor adjudged them to be sent to District Court holden at Winchester, for further trial."
(Winchester Gazette)[43]

---

[43] *Maryland Herald and Weekly Advertiser* on Microfilm January 14, 1803, Page 3-D. Washington Co. (MD) Free Library.

At a Superior Court, held in and for the District composed of the Counties of Frederick, Berkeley, Shenandoah and Jefferson in the Commonwealth of Virginia, held at Winchester on Friday the 15th of April, 1803. Present: Joseph Jones and Robert White, Jr., Judges of the General Court. A Grand Jury was convened of which Lawrence Butler was Foreman and after hearing the testimony returned an indictment against all four men jointly and individually in the Felony of Counterfeiting the hard currency of the United States of America of base metal in the similarity of the silver dollars of the Mint Emission of 1795 to 1798.

The trials of these men came on the 16th and 17th of April, 1803, with three of the four found guilty as charged of Felony Counterfeiting. Thomas Cumsey was sentenced to four years at hard labor or in solitary confinement; Francis Streithoff, blacksmith, to four years at hard labor or in solitary confinement and to be placed on a low and coarse diet for one-fourth part of these four years, both to pay a fine and both to be confined in the Jail and Penitentiary House.

Valentine Shockey was sentenced on May 23, 1803, in which the Court, after some post-trial investigation said, "That said Valentine Shockey should undergo a confinement of six years at hard labour (sic) or in solitude and that he be placed in the solitary cells of the Jail and Penitentiary House in Richmond and that he be placed on a low and coarse diet during one-third part of the said six years and that he make a fine of twenty-dollars with his Excellency John Page, Esq.,

Governor of the Commonwealth. And the Court doth report to the inspector of the Penitentiary, that from the testimony upon the trial of said Valentine Shockey, it appears...the said Shockey is a man of infamous character, but, that it does not appear to them that he was ever before convicted of any felony or other infamous crime whatsoever and...the said Valentine Shockey is remanded to be conducted to said Jail and Penitentiary House by the Sheriff of Frederick County."[44]

The Jail and Penitentiary House in Richmond was practically brand new, having been built in 1800, and was a precursor of many of its type in the United States. We experimented with freedom, so did we with punishment, and we continue to experiment today with both concepts.

The solitary cells at Richmond Penitentiary measured 3½ feet wide by 7 feet long by 7 feet high. A day at hard labor would be preferred to solitary confinement in such a space!

Valentine Shockey was sixty-four years old when he entered there. It is likely that there he ended his days. It was said that those who did not die there, most certainly went insane! Virginia laws concerned with counterfeiting were lenient by most standards and the days of the death penalty were limited. Ohio in 1788 and Pennsylvania in 1794 were first to limit the death penalty to the crime of murder alone.

This is but an attempt to separate the reality from the myth of the fabled counterfeiters of the South Mountain and I am sure there is more to be told.

---

[44] Order Book #51 Superior Court of Frederick County, Virginia 1803-1807, Clerk of the Courts Office, Court House, Winchester, VA.

Smithsonian Institution-National Numismatic Collection PHOTO

Genuine US 1795-98 Silver Dollar

Shockey, Streithoff & Co. were probably striking this type coin when they were apprehended at the, blacksmith shop in Sleepy Creek, VA. (Now W. Va)

William Butler Yeats once said, "There is some Myth for every man, which, if we but knew it; it would make us understand all that he did and thought."

Oh! I almost forgot! That den was finally found, although all that is left of it is the opening. The larger part of it had been blasted by the County Commissioners during the years of Prohibition of alcohol to make it inaccessible to bootleggers. It was once a great tourist attraction and had been exploited as such by the summer resorts in the Blue Ridge Summit area. It had a path to it and a directional sign and was a great place for "spooners." It was located in Washington County, Maryland, and we are in luck in having a description of it from the April 20, 1891 issue of *The Hagerstown Daily Mail*.

> "Saturday, two gentlemen, one of this and one rather more familiar with the mountain paths, started out from the new Buena Vista Hotel determined to search for the place. They paced back along the stream until they came to an old path in the wilderness. They scrambled along the path and came to a narrow slit in a massive rock, thickly surrounded by bushes and trees.
>
> They squeezed into the place and came to a sudden falling off and came out and tried it backwards. When they reached the ground, they found themselves in a narrow hall capable of being defended against an army, and with a breastwork at the end. They crawled over this and went on and at a turn walked into a room fully 40 feet by 40 feet and with a ceiling of about 10 feet high. Here one of the explorers picked up a brass revolutionary soldier button. The room was bare.
>
> Through a narrow doorway they pierced into a smaller room with a lofty ceiling and in the rear of this another room with a

stream of water rushing through it. Here, doubtless, was the distillery part of the cave, but nothing whatever was found.

The young man who lived on the mountain showed the Hagerstown man some old time dies and stamps that he said he has taken from the place.

It is said that the company building the hotel (Buena Vista Hotel) will use the cave as a show place, arch the opening and build a stairway to facilitate the inspection of it."

Entrance to Shockey's Cave

Not actually a cave, but an opening in the boulders. The chasm was blasted during the 1920 prohibition years to deter moonshining. Thus ended its illicit use as a hideout for over 150 years. The entrance extends a mere 10 or 15 feet deep and appears today as shown here.